ASIAN RURAL SOCIETY
CHINA, INDIA, JAPAN

ASIAN
RURAL SOCIETY
CHINA, INDIA, JAPAN

TADASHI FUKUTAKE
University of Tokyo

UNIVERSITY OF WASHINGTON PRESS
SEATTLE AND LONDON

Published in Japan by
University of Tokyo Press
Hongo, Tokyo, Japan
with the assistance of
The Publication Fund of the Ministry of Education

To
My Foreign Friends

PREFACE

I have collected in this volume several survey reports and some of my more theoretical writings concerning villages in China, India, and Japan. The essays span a period of some twenty years. The chapters on China were written immediately after the war and describe wartime conditions, while the discussion of Indian villages deals with the contemporary scene. The chapters on Japan cover both the immediate postwar situation and the tremendous and rapid changes of recent years.

The fact that, however lacking they may be in theoretical unity, these essays do at least cover the three major countries of Asia is due more than anything else to the accident of the author's own personal history. After I graduated from the University of Tokyo in 1940, I was able to spend several spring and summer vacations travelling to China, particularly central China, for field work in rural villages. Although it was wartime, the farmers of the villages we visited accepted the fact that we were brought there by academic curiosity and treated us with a friendliness which it is even now pleasant to recall. It was not a happy situation, however. Being in my early twenties and no lover of the army and its wars, I could not help but be conscious of the suffering which Japanese aggression was bringing to the people of China. To plunge into Chinese village life and concentrate single-mindedly on the collection of facts was perhaps something of an escape.

When the war was brought to an end by Japan's defeat, my own studies of China also perforce came to an end. From then on it became my principal concern to investigate the villages of my own country. It was a fascinating study at a fascinating time, made the more interesting as the Chinese villages provided for me an implicit point of comparison. For the immediate postwar years I devoted all my energy to the study of Japanese rural society.

It was not until 1959 that I turned again to the outside world.

The World Congress of Sociology, held in Italy that year, gave me the chance to spend a short week in the Italian countryside and another in rural France. In 1960 and 1961 a UNESCO fellowship made it possible for me to visit villages in India and America. I learned a lot from both countries, especially from my stay in an American farmhouse, but it was Indian village society and its contrast with China which particularly fascinated me. I was anxious to return, and in the winter of 1962 I was able to persuade Professor Tsutomu Ouchi, an agricultural economist, and Professor Chie Nakane, a social anthropologist, to accompany me on a two-month survey of two Indian villages. My main interest was to see how Indian rural society, with a family structure in many ways similar to that of China, nevertheless differed because of the caste system. Back in Japan, I turned again to the study of Japanese villages and the processes of social change which have become so marked in recent years. At that time I wrote an introductory outline study of village society in Japan, primarily with a view to its being translated and read by my foreign friends. The translation, under the title *Japanese Rural Society*, is being published by the Oxford University Press.

The present volume springs also from the desire to share my findings and ideas with, and to evoke reactions from, colleagues in the field of rural sociology in other countries. It consists of some essays and reports which had already been translated into English, together with two or three which are here translated for the first time. For the lack of systematic unity and adequate comparative analysis in the contents, the responsibility is mine, not that of the many friends who assisted me in its preparation, as they did my former collection of essays, *Man and Society in Japan*. The introduction was translated by Professor Ronald Dore of the London School of Economics and I owe to Dr. John McEwan the accurate translation of the chapters on India. The chapters on Japanese and Chinese villages were in part translated or edited by Professor Harumi Befu of Stanford University, the translation staff of *Japan Quarterly*, and Professor Robert A. Polson of Cornell University. I am grateful, too, for the assistance of Miss Miriam Brokaw of Princeton University Press during her year as visiting editor with the University of Tokyo Press, and of Miss Ellen Logan who succeeded her and assisted the editing of the manuscript. My grateful thanks also go to

Professor Megumi Hayashi with whom I did the field work in China, to Professors Tsutomu Ouchi and Chie Nakane who worked with me in the Indian villages, and also to all those who have made my research on Japanese villages possible.

July 1966
Tokyo   TADASHI FUKUTAKE

CONTENTS

PART II   SURVEY REPORTS

MAPS

PLATES

TABLES

ASIAN RURAL SOCIETY
China, India, Japan

INTRODUCTION

The collection together of essays on villages in China, India, and Japan should obviously provide the opportunity for a wide-ranging exercise in comparative sociology. Unfortunately, I find myself unequal to the task. The book does contain one essay which attempts a comparison between Chinese and Japanese villages, but I find that my memories of China twenty years ago and my impressions of a shorter, recent visit to India do not form the basis for a systematic attack on the potentially more interesting comparison between India and China. The best I can do in this introduction is to offer a few impressions and to pose a few questions.

Rural Society in the Three Countries

A hundred years ago all three countries were agricultural societies with no important industry besides agriculture. Their development over the last century has brought great differences, transforming Japan through the rapid development of a capitalist economy from an agricultural into an industrial nation. In agricultural production too the steady increase in Japan contrasts with stagnation in China and in India. If one compares them in the immediate prewar period, Chinese agriculture was approximately at the level of productivity achieved by Japan at the time of the Meiji Restoration of 1868, while India's production levels were about equal to those of Japan in the Tokugawa period.

How does one explain this? Climatic and soil conditions may be part of the explanation. It is doubtless important too that their encounter with the West took different forms: India was colonized and China semi-colonized while Japan escaped subordination. At the same time we must not overlook the importance of the differences in their pre-modern societies. Here again the effect of differing geographical circumstances cannot be ignored, but it is important that Japan had a feudal system similar to that found in

Europe, whereas neither China nor India had anything which could strictly be called feudal as the term is normally used. Under Japanese feudalism, Japanese farmers were able to support large numbers of feudal lords and their samurai retainers—one important indication that Japan's level of agricultural productivity was higher than that of either China or India. As a result of this feudal system, moreover, I think one can say that Japanese village society acquired a different character from that of the other two countries.

Japan, unlike China or India, did not have a system of equal division of inheritance among sons. The Japanese *dōzoku* system of extended family relations differed from the Chinese clan or the Indian *gotra*. China and India were also similar in practising clan exogamy, though India has the unique feature of strictly enforcing caste endogamy. What is the reason for these differences? The difference between a China created by the Han people and an India in which an Aryan people imposed themselves on a number of subsidiary tribes must form the basis of any explanation of the differences between China and India; as between Japan and both of these countries, however, the great influence of the feudal system on Japan's family structure has to be taken into account. The question of why there was clan exogamy in China but not in Japan remains one that is worth pursuing, although I cannot go into it here.

see pg. 86 ?

There are also differences in village structure. Because the principle of primogeniture succession held in Japan, the ruling stratum of a village tended to be comparatively stable over the generations. This stability was lacking in China and India. In China the non-cultivating landlord gentry showed some stability, but they were above, not of, the farming class. In India there was as in China no continuity of stable power for particular families, although in caste terms the dominant caste did not easily lose its supremacy. It is also relevant that in Japan the leading families in the village were tied to the poorer peasants by bonds of paternalistic familism. This is a feature absent in the other two countries where one does not find the peculiarly Japanese practice of incorporating unrelated servant families as "branch families" into the clan. As a consequence, land-lord-tenant relations in China and India tended to become nakedly exploitative, and lacking in any of the effective elements of protection and service.

There are also differences in the relation between power in the village system and power in the national system. In Japan it was rare for the ruling stratum of the villages to enhance its powers of exploiting the peasants by virtue of its links with national political power. In China, by contrast, the landlord-gentry class provided the society's intellectuals and, at the same time, the nation's officials, so that its national political position reinforced its local power. In India the zamindari system operated in a similar way, but the discrimination of human worth implied in the caste system probably gave an extra cutting edge to the upper castes' exploitation of the lower castes and untouchables with results that were worse than in China. The caste system also deserves study as a factor in the stagnation of Indian society and in this connection there may be an instructive comparison between the dissolution of the Tokugawa status system in the Japan of the Meiji period and the persistance of the Indian caste system until the present day.

How do these characteristics of Japanese rural society relate to the fact that Japan is an exception among the so-called "stagnant oriental societies" in developing a capitalist economy? This is an interesting question to which it is not easy to give a simple answer. Agriculture certainly supported the early stages of capitalist development but this is not the only aspect of the matter. The special social characteristics of Japanese villages also offered favorable factors for Japan's industrialization. The absence of divided inheritance in Japan meant that as soon as there were opportunities for younger sons to move out of agriculture, these opportunities were fully utilized. Migration was steady and rapid, and as the younger sons manned the new industries, their elder brothers who inherited the family property were able to supplement the workers' low industrial wages, at least in emergencies. This feature is not unconnected with the rapid rate of capital accumulation in industry. Again the nature of the relationship between the ruling stratum of villagers and the mass of poorer peasants—on the one hand economic exploitation through a high level of rents and on the other their social imprisonment in the affective bonds of paternalistic familism—lent stability to rural society and aided the development of industry. The relative absence of politically effective demands from the peasants for state investment in the modernization of agriculture meant that the state had the necessary maneuverability to concentrate on the protection and encouragement of industry.

These factors may well have helped the speedy growth of the Japanese economy, but they did nothing to prevent Japan's taking the path of imperialistic conquest. The familism of the Japanese village was linked with the familistic character of the Japanese state of which the Emperor was the supreme patriarch, and the farmers found no difficulty in accepting the state's expansionist policies. Although up to a certain point the traditional characteristics of Japanese society operated as factors favorable to progress, they needed amendment in a modern direction if they were thenceforth to contribute to normal development. And if one is to ask why they were not amended, the explanation must at least go back to the differing characteristics of Japanese and European feudalism. Whereas the feudal bond in the west had something of the character of a mutual contract ("If the lord does not behave like a lord, the retainer has no obligation to act as a retainer"), in Japan the emphasis was on unilateral obligations ("Even if the lord does not behave like a lord, the retainer must always be a loyal retainer"). At this point, in other words, comparisons with Europe become more relevant than comparisons among Asian countries.

Post-war Changes in Perspective

The occasion for altering the traditional character of Japanese society finally came at the end of the second world war when Japan was under the control of a Western occupying army.

In the early stages of the development of Japan's capitalist economy the rural landlord class produced many able and talented men, and I have already referred to the function of the landlords as a stabilizing power in the villages preventing the overt expression of peasant discontent towards state policies favoring industrial development. But this is also to say, put the other way round, that they impeded the democratic development of rural society. And yet, as the development of the economy increased the relative power of the industrial capitalists and reduced that of the landlords, rural society itself began slowly to change.

These changes revealed themselves in the decisive transformations which occurred in the post-war period. The first victims of the drive to rebuild Japan's post-war economy were the already weakened landlords. Their power disintegrated in the land reform which, under the surveillance of the occupation army, was carried out with more thoroughness than in any other free enterprise economy. Nevertheless, this was still a reform and not a revolution. Agriculture made progress as a result of the land reform, but as the effects of the infinitely greater growth of industry began to make themselves felt, the limitations of the reform became apparent and the search began for new approaches. I have described these processes in the essay "Changing Japanese Rural Society" which has been included in this volume.

Post-war China, by contrast, experienced a Communist revolution. It is not difficult to see how conditions for revolutionary change were present in Chinese villages. Where the relations between the landlords and the cultivating peasants were not characterized by the familistic paternalism common in Japan, a radical revolution could more easily be carried through; while for peasants of low productivity, living in miserable poverty, the prospect—or at least the possibility—of any improvement in production and income provided adequate motive for supporting the reform. At the same time there were few barriers to revolutionary indoctrination among peasants of low educational levels, little given to self-reliant individualism. These circumstances made possible the radical Communist transformation of the countryside through cooperatives to communes within the space of a decade.

In a sense the path taken by Indian rural society in the post-war years may be said to lie between that of China and Japan—in the sense, that is, that while Japan remains a capitalist country and China has become a Communist one, India proclaims itself Socialist. That socialism, however, remains little more than a label or an aspiration. And this is particularly marked with regard to the land question which in India was resolved by a land reform far less thorough than Japan's. The area which landlords were allowed to retain was large and consequently the proportion of land redistributed small; caste differences and differences in landed property still tend to correlate. Caste discrimination has been officially outlawed but remains in practice. As I have argued in the essay "Change and Stagnation in the Indian Village," despite the great change represented by post-war independence, the traditional character of Indian village society seems to have been little altered.

What forecasts can one make about future trends in the rural areas of these three countries? In Japan the agricultural population has already declined to European levels and further decreases can be expected. The result will be further social change in the rural areas, but it seems that as long as the structure of Japanese politics remains unchanged, the major result will be a steady increase in part-time farming rather than the development of a new type of village. The prospects are not good for agriculture to become a profitable enterprise, to be chosen as an occupation rather than inherited as a way of life. New directions are unlikely to emerge until, with the change of generations and the gradual acceptance of the new Civil Code's provisions for equal inheritance, the demand for an agriculture productive enough to bring about equal inheritance transforms itself into a politically effective force. And for such a pattern of agriculture to be possible, some form of socialist policy will probably be necessary.

In China we are likely to see a continuation of Communist policies and an increase in agricultural productivity. Since there is no reason to foresee a slackening in the process of Communist "human reconstruction," it will probably be a long time before Chinese farmers are permitted the luxury of freedom of thought. But the fact that they are subject to Communist indoctrination and that the day when they are freed from strict controls is likely to be distant is not as tragic for Chinese farmers as people in other countries might think. To consider then equally as unfortunate as the victims of Fascist oppression is to betray an unnecessary solicitude, natural only to the inhabitants of those countries for whom free competition *does* mean the enjoyment of a high standard of living. One can expect Chinese farmers to be satisfied with a gradual rise in their real levels of living and to cooperate energetically in the building of a Communist state. Freedom will become an issue for them after the foundations of the new state are firmly laid.

As for India, my essay in this volume argues that Indian villages have a good deal to learn from China. In such matters as the spread of education the Japanese example may have something to teach, but it is my belief that Japan's choice of the capitalist path of development cannot provide a model for India. Such techniques as the "Japanese method" of rice growing apart, a country with even lower levels of productivity than China will be forced, in my view, to allow the drive to raise agricultural productivity take precedence over the development of heavy industry, and in this respect India cannot follow the path of Japan in over-hasty industrialization. The socialism which has been India's proclaimed objective should not be allowed to remain an empty slogan; unless it is carried into practice, no fundamental change in village society is likely. And it is difficult to escape the conclusion that as long as there is evasion of a direct attack on the caste system there can be no true socialism in India.

These questions of the future are not easy and admit of no simple answers. My treatment of them may be too bold or even fundamentally misconceived. Nevertheless I do believe that comparisons can be instructive and that we can learn from each other while acknowledging that every country must choose its own path, and that while there may be certain problems that are common to comparable stages of economic development the special social characteristics of each society impose important limiting conditions.

Looked at with these problems in mind, this volume represents a most feeble contribution to their resolution. But if, in spite of the slightness of its substantive contribution, it can stimulate scholars in other countries to further and more satisfactory comparative analysis, and if it can provide them with some of the material for doing so, my purpose in compiling it will have been achieved.

PART I
THEORETICAL ESSAYS

1. CHINESE VILLAGE AND JAPANESE VILLAGE

The character of rural society differs significantly in Asia and the West. Although agriculture no longer dominates production in modern capitalistic society, it affected the initial development of modern capitalism as well as its subsequent progress. In Asia, where modern capitalism remains relatively retarded and where the agricultural population is still large, many of the factors delaying Asia's modernization may be found in the character of the farming villages. Study of the Asian farming village is, therefore, a prerequisite for understanding modernization in Asian society.

Although China and Japan are geographically Asian, the two countries are quite dissimilar. Since the factors which distinguish them may be seen first in the agricultural sphere, we will limit this paper to a comparison of rural villages in China and Japan. Lack of space precludes reference to every type of village in both countries and we will be able to discuss only the most typical characteristics. The formation of these characteristics and the reasons for their respective differences also fall outside the scope of this introductory paper. What will be said in conclusion is a tentative hypothesis for further investigation.

I. CHARACTERISTICS OF THE FAMILY

In villages without the capitalistic management of agriculture, the family is a consumptive as well as a productive unit. The family is, generally, far more important in rural areas than in cities, and where villages are composed of small farmers, as in China or Japan, the role of the family assumes even greater significance. The first step in a comparative sociological analysis, therefore, is to examine family characteristics.

This essay contrasts the pre-World War II village of China and Japan. It was written in 1948.

The rural family, both in China and Japan, is patriarchal, but many differences may be recorded within a patriarchal family structure, as was pointed out by K. A. Wittfogel.[1] The Chinese family includes more collateral relatives than the Japanese family.[2] In Japan, second and third sons usually leave the family after marriage. In China, junior sons often live in the home with the eldest son during the parents' lifetime. Although co-residence of married brothers is, in fact, difficult and they eventually separate, the traditional ideal remains that the family property should not be divided before the parents' death; thus, the *dōzoku* (clan) family type in Eitaro Suzuki's sense occurs more frequently in China than in Japan.[3]

Patriarchal authority appears stronger in Japan; the Japanese rural family head retains strong authority even toward collateral members. The eldest brother as the heir to the family can control his younger brothers' behavior. In China, the authority of the family head toward collateral members is considerably attenuated but remains strong toward lineal descendants since the authority of the family head and that of the father are combined in the same person.

In China it is assumed that sooner or later the family property will be divided equally, while in Japan, the house property is thought to belong to the family unit which continues in direct succession to the main family. The feeling of inheriting family property from one's ancestors is particularly strong in Japan. The Chinese idea of common ownership of family property makes those who live and work away from home obliged to send money to the family. Japanese younger sons are under no such obligation, unless their parents and family remaining at home are in dire need.

The most obvious difference between the two societies is seen in the manner of inheritance. In China, family property is always

[1] K. A. Wittfogel, "Wirtschaftliche Grundlagen der Entwichlung der Familienautorität," *Studien über Autorität und Familie*, Schriften des Instituts für Sozialforschung, Bd. 5, 1936, S. 511f.

[2] See Tatsumi Makino, "A Comparison of Family Composition in China and Japan," *Shina Kazoku Kenkyū* (Studies on the Chinese Family), Tokyo: Seikatsusha, 1944, pp. 619ff.

[3] Eitaro Suzuki, *Nihon Nōson Shakaigaku Genri* (Principles of Japanese Rural Sociology), Tokyo: Jichōsha, 1940, p. 172. Incidentally, Suzuki considers the Chinese village an intermediate type between the Japanese and the Western village (Ibid., p. 7); but his point cannot be readily accepted.

divided equally among male family members. This division might be better described as partition than as inheritance.[4] In Japan, the priority of inheritance is placed on the succession to the family headship; thus, inheritance preferentially favors the eldest son in the direct line. The Chinese feel that the inheritance of the duties of family rituals and festivals are relatively unimportant and, generally, no special rights and duties are associated with the eldest son's position. The Chinese make a funeral service as grand as possible for their parents but this obligation is shared equally among the sons. If property partition occurs while the parents are living, the Chinese care for them in any number of ways, none of which are common in Japan. Such practices include setting aside land for the parents' exclusive use, contributing an equal amount of food and money for their use, or giving them lodging in one's home on a rotational basis. The Japanese family maintains clear distinctions between the eldest son, the heir to the family, and the second, third, or younger sons. In China, where each son has equal property rights, there is no rule of family succession by the eldest son.

In short, the Chinese family, based on the idea of common property ownership, is united just as strongly as the Japanese family, but the custom of sharing the family inheritance on an equal basis tends to diffuse solidarity. In China, therefore, when married brothers live together, family stability is low; for although the extended family system is more common in China than in Japan, strictly equal contribution by all family members is difficult to achieve. In Japan, the eldest son is considered from birth as heir to the family and younger sons are regarded as hangers-on, subordinate to their eldest brother. The division of the family estate in China is a partition of a house into equal parts, while establishment of a branch family in Japan is considered a reward given to junior sons for their service to the parent house.

---

[4] See the review of the author's *Chūgoku Nōson-shakai no Kōzō* (The Structure of Chinese Rural Society), Kyoto: Taigadō, 1946, by Noboru Niida in *Teikoku Daigaku Shinbun* (The Imperial University Journal), No. 1011, Jan. 22, 1947; Noboru Niida, "On Family Disorganization in Northern Chinese Villages," *Tōyō Bunka Kenkyū* (Journal of Asian Culture), No. 4, June 1947; Michitaka Kaino, *Hokushi Nōson ni okeru Kankō Gaisetsu* (Introduction to Village Customs in Northern China), Tōa Kenkyūsho (The Research Institute on East Asia), Research Materials I, No. 37C, 1944, p. 34.

II. Structure of the Clan

Differences in family system are further reflected in the structure of the clan—the Chinese *tsungtsu* or the Japanese *dōzoku*. The importance of the clan in village life underlines the significance of its structure in a comparative study of village social characteristics.

In the Chinese village the eldest male member of the oldest generation in the *tsungtsu* usually becomes the clan chief, except in some parts of southern China where a priestly status is recognized for the lineal descendants of the principal family. As a rule, the clan chief does not come from one particular family nor is he the most powerful member of the clan. He may sometimes come from a poor family and have no prestige with which to control the clan; in such cases, larger clans appoint influential and intelligent individuals as clan officials, regardless of their clan branch. In Japan, the chief must come from the main family; his age is irrelevant. The main family as a corporate entity supervises all the events of the *dōzoku*, particularly the clan rituals and festivals.

In organization, the Chinese *tsungtsu* operates on a generation basis, and gives priority to the oldest generation. Age is emphasized after generation. During ritual occasions, for example, one must pay proper respect to a member of an older generation even if he is younger and comes from a distant collateral family. The Japanese *dōzoku* is organized on a main-branch house relationship; each family is incorporated within a hierarchy according to its respective time of branching and genealogical distance from the main line. The greatest importance is placed upon the hierarchical relationship of the main family, the branches, and the latter's branches. In the Chinese village, aside from considerations of generation and age, every member of the *tsungtsu* is equal.

The Chinese *tsungtsu* possesses a certain amount of clan property, although not so much as is popularly imagined. The clan's resources are reserved for festivals and rituals and for financial assistance to its members. The Japanese *dōzoku* owns no comparable property, but the estate of the main family fulfills a similar function. A prosperous main family will bear the expense of festivals and rituals as well as offer financial assistance to its members. Even when the main family is not wealthy, it is expected to bear more expense than the branch families.

The Chinese *tsungtsu* system is based on patrilineal descent and prohibits adoption from outside the clan. Although matrilocal marriage is possible in the absence of a male heir, the proper succession-procedure requires adoption of the family chief's brother's son. In Japan, marriage into the family of an heiress is a common practice. Before the enforcement of the Meiji Civil Code, if a family's first child was female and no male child was close to her in age, the family could adopt a man from outside the family to be the daughter's husband and the inheritor of the family property; the family could then set up a branch family for the son or send him out for adoption. The rather common occurrence of these practices indicate that the principle of agnatic succession is not strictly observed in Japan. Furthermore, while members of the same *tsungtsu* do not intermarry in China, intermarriage within the clan is permitted in Japan and is encouraged as a means of strengthening the exclusive ties common to the *dōzoku*. Significantly, blood ties are de-emphasized in the Japanese *dōzoku* since the main-branch family relationship is a vertical relationship like that of a master and servant and, as such, allows the establishment of branch families headed by non-blood relations. This contrasts sharply with the closed kinship structure of the Chinese *tsungtsu*.

The emphasis placed on generations in the Chinese clan tends to make it unstable and the traditional authority accorded to the clan chief does not include *de facto* control of the clan. In principle, each family in the clan stands on an equal footing, but the family which has the most power at any one time influences the clan and a handful of able clansmen can practically control the entire clan. In Japan, the main family derives its authority from its lineal descent and maintains its traditional authority through the support of the branch families. A typical *dōzoku* exists to maintain and solidify the main family; the main family thus served and supported obliges itself to protect and aid its branches.

The data we collected did not make patently clear the relative intensity of clan solidarity in China and Japan, but to postulate the stronger solidarity of clan sentiment in China on the basis of property or shrines held in common would be overhasty.[5] The signifi-

[5] See Noboru Niida, *Shina Mibunhōshi* (A History of Chinese Civil Code), Tokyo: Tōhōbunka Kenkyūsho, 1942, p. 174. See also Michitaka Kaino, *Hōritsu-shakaigaku no Shomondai* (Problems in the Sociology of Law), Tokyo: Nihonhyōronsha, 1943, pp. 141–2.

cance of clan property, clan genealogical records, and clan shrines may be interpreted as means to prevent that dispersion of the clan which would result from an equal division of property. Needless to say, the *tsungtsu's* emphasis of exogamy makes its members more aware of the clan and its boundaries than does the *dōzoku* with its more casual attitude toward blood relationships. However, in the typical Japanese village where the *dōzoku* is united by a main family-centered ideology and the relationship between the main and branch families is predicated upon a master-servant relationship, clan solidarity is stronger than in the Chinese village.

III. STRATIFICATION IN THE VILLAGE

Villages in China and Japan are thus composed of different types of families and clan groups. Differences in the village structure as a unit will now be examined on the basis of differences in kinship.

The average cultivated land per household is approximately one *chō*[6] in Japan, and about 18 *mu*[6] in China. Since the rice yield in China averages about 65 per cent of the Japanese yield, the economic condition of a Chinese farmer is below that of his Japanese neighbor. Although a completely accurate comparison is impossible here, the findings of the Fifth Committee of the Research Institute on East Asia reveal the following facts on China: the average area of cultivated land is 112 per cent that of Japan's; the average crop of unpolished rice is 66 per cent (or 25 per cent in terms of price); gross income is 28 per cent and net income (gross income minus capital investment and rent) comes up to 43 per cent. (The relatively high net income depends upon lower capital expenses and rents in China.)[7] Although not completely reliable, the findings of the Research Institute certainly indicate that both agricultural techniques and the economy are less developed in China than in Japan.

Because of the high proportion of petty farmers, class composition appears similar in both countries, but if we consider the data mentioned above, the number of economically deprived farmers is larger

[6] One *chō* is 2.45 acres; one *mu* is .16 acres.

[7] The figures in *Shina Inasaku-Nōkakeizai no Kichō* (The Basis of Rice-producing Farm Economy in China), Report of the Research Institute on East Asia, Tokyo, No. 14, 1942.

in China. Stratification trends in Japan indicate that farm house-holds cultivating from one to three *chō* are relatively stable (this should not be interpreted, however, as an increase in the number of middle class farmers). In China the trend is toward an increase in the percentage of petty and poor farmers who are ignored by upper class farmers and further abandoned by the village community.

The best available statistics on China show that owner-tenant farmers constitute 24 per cent and tenant farmers 29 per cent of the total number of farmers—thus lease-holding farmers total 53 per cent.[8] In Japan, owner-tenants constitute 38 per cent and tenants 29 per cent, a total of 67 per cent, making the rate of tenancy higher in Japan than in China.[9] Although tenancy is significant in both countries, tenancy in China is contractual and does not normally include any duties beyond payment of the rent. In Japan, the rela-tionship between landlord and tenant (when both live in the same area) involves personal considerations and assumes the form of a parent-child relationship. Gradually disappearing, this type of paternalistic relationship to one's tenant still occurs in modern Japan. The term of tenancy is usually indefinite in both China and Japan, but in Japan an implicit agreement for an indefinite period often manifests itself in a guise of parent-child loyalty, as has been pointed out by Kizaemon Ariga.[10]

This type of parent-child relationship ties the poorer farmers to the wealthy, upper-class farmer group. In China, however, the farmers have no such social relationship, and the mass of poverty-stricken farmers remains isolated from the wealthy landlord group. The Chinese type of class structure promotes exploitation and hos-tility among the classes. Japanese class relationships are supple-mented by social ties of a familial nature which reduce or eliminate the likelihood of an exploitative economic relationship. Upper and lower strata are bound by main-branch family ties as well as by master-servant relationships. Such relationships are commonly found in Japanese villages but rarely in China, where parent-child

[8] Central Laboratory of Agriculture, The Government of China, *Report on Agricultural Conditions*, Vol. 5, No. 1, Nangking, 1937.

[9] Nōrinshō Tōkeika (Statistics Section of the Ministry of Agriculture and Forestry), *Nōrin Tōkei Geppō* (Monthly Report on Agricultural Statistics), No. 91, 1946.

[10] Kizaemon Ariga, *Nihon Kazoku-seido to Kosaku-seido* (The Japanese Family System and the Tenancy System), Tokyo: Kawadeshobō, 1943, pp. 701–4.

adoption is practiced only as a superstitious means of altering a child's inauspicious circumstances.

Class division in the Chinese village, therefore, hampers social integration. The comparatively low economic conditions in China drive the mass of petty and poor farmers out of village social life, while there are few farmers in Japan so destitute, *i.e.*, so without aid from the upper farmer group, their paternalistic masters, that they cannot participate in village affairs.

IV. CHARACTERISTICS OF THE VILLAGE

Chinese villages as a unit own very little property. Village shrines may own a few rice fields. Occasionally, villages own their own forest and pasture land, graveyards, agricultural tools, and even fishing rights to rivers and ponds, but these properties do not appreciably benefit the entire village. Most Japanese villages, on the other hand, own communal forest and pasture lands, and although community consciousness has declined since World War II, the farmers' awareness of village-owned property strengthens their community spirit.

In general, an individual's awareness of village borders is ill-defined in China; areas where the lands owned by farmers of one village adjoin those of neighboring villages are vaguely accepted as the borderlines. Chinese villages are traditionally organized not on a geographical basis but in terms of household units. In Japan, village borders are clearly delineated, for the feudal taxation system required well-defined fiscal units which in turn fostered the strong village consciousness that still exists today.

A further difference appears in the villagers' attitude toward the village shrine. For example, the Japanese village shrine is worshiped by villagers as if they all belonged to one clan, as the Japanese clan has always been considered a more important territorial than kinship group. Occasionally, a clan god became the local village deity and a tutelary deity may thereby combine the characteristics of ancestral and local deity. In China the village shrine and the clan-ancestral shrine have never been combined and stand as two different institutions.[11] Referring to the Chinese practice of reporting vil-

[11] This kind of dualistic division is also reported in Kulp's study of a southern Chinese village. D. H. Kulp, *Country Life in South China: The Sociology of Familism,*

lagers' deaths to the earth-god, R. F. Johnston insisted on a common origin for the Chinese earth-god shrine and the Japanese village shrine,[12] but this is incorrect. The Japanese villagers do not report anyone's death to a shrine, whose purpose is to avert death and perpetuate life. The Chinese clan shrine does memorialize all *tungtsu* members after their death, but village gods and shrines in the two countries are quite different.

The separation of village and clan shrines in China implies a factor which works against village unity. This may be traced back to the character of the Chinese clan, based exclusively on kinship, which prevents an openness seen in the Japanese *dōzoku*; different kinship clans in the same village rarely cooperate and often come into open conflict. In Japan, where several *dōzoku* groups coexist, the less influential groups subjugate themselves to the powerful *dōzoku* group in a master-servant relationship. Thus, *dōzoku* ties are integrated into village ties, a combination which works to concentrate village authority in the main family of one powerful clan.

V. AUTONOMY IN THE VILLAGE

The Chinese village, reflecting the class division mentioned earlier, benefits principally the rich landowner class. The village lacks communal financial strength; political interest lags and little is done for the betterment of village life. This is best illustrated by the example of the crop-watching association of the north Chinese village.[13] The association, an official village agency, functions in the interest of the landowning class by preventing crimes of larceny by destitute farmers. The association chief is always selected from among the wealthy landowners and without the consent of the poor farmers.

New York: Teachers College (Columbia University), 1925. See also Yoshitarō Hirano, *Hokushi Sonraku no Kōsei-yōso to shite no Kazoku oyobi Sonbyō* (The Family and Village Shrine as Basic Features of the Northern Chinese Village), *Shina Nōson Kankō Chōsa* (Research Report on Chinese Rural Customs), RIEA Research Materials, No. 25C, 1943, p. 27ff.

[12] R. F. Johnston, *Lion and Dragon in Northern China*, London: J. Murray, 1910, pp. 372–3.

[13] "The fundamental task of the crop-watching association clearly indicates the locus of power in village politics." Morimitsu Shimizu, *Shina Shakai no Kenkyū* (A Study of Chinese Society), Tokyo: Iwanami-shoten, 1939, p. 297.

The *de facto* ruler of the Chinese village tends to avoid becoming its administrative chief. Administrative responsibilities including police, land survey, registration, and tax work are traditionally regarded as responsibilities below the level of the gentry. For this reason, a distinction between the natural village and the administrative village still exists. The village administrators depend upon the support of the upper classes and are subject to their influence. Power is monopolized by private individuals and bribery is common. Even if the *de facto* ruler becomes the village administrator, the situation remains the same. These administrators, if they are formally elected, rarely have the positive support of the poor villagers. They therefore feel little involvement in the village as a whole and, although village officials, are primarily interested in private power. Thus the control exercised by the village officials depends upon their own and the upper classes' economic power; the only real difference between ruler and ruled is economic power. The submission of the lower classes is never rooted in their trust of the village administrators, and they feel the absence of a representative leadership concerned with the welfare and protection of the total village.[14]

Japanese village leaders under the rule of the Tokugawa shogunate felt a personal obligation, as village representatives, to protect the common interests of all villagers, rich and poor, from the oppression of the feudal lord. Naturally, the leaders themselves were somewhat ambitious, but their ambition was tempered by a very real responsibility to the villagers who regarded them as parents. Thus, in Japan, representatives and represented were bound by a parent-child relationship. The real chief and the formal chief were usually the same person, since those with high social status always become village representatives. Various feudal conditions maintained the family status of these village leaders, and they derived and preserved their traditional authority from their status as *dōzoku* leaders or *oyakata*, *i.e.*, patriarchal masters. Simultaneously, the economic power of the leadership group allowed it to exert strong and unified control over the village through its management of communal property and through village solidarity expressed symbolically in the village shrine. Since the Meiji Restoration, new

[14] For information on the village ruling group, see M. C. Young, *A Chinese Village*, London: Kegan Paul, 1947, Chapter 14.

economic and administrative policies have transformed the traditional Tokugawa system, although elements of its political system
still persist. New municipal offices handle the former administrative functions of the Tokugawa village, yet the old principle of service and protection remains intact in the interdependent relationship
of ruled and ruler, extending at times into the political structure
of the administrative village.[15]

Thus, communal autonomy in the Chinese village is inactive and
negative. Repair of roads or construction of irrigation systems is
hardly a village-wide task; community assistance is rarely given to
destitute farmers even after natural calamities. "In ordinary times,
little or nothing is done, it is only when some emergency occurs . . .
and consequently, nothing is done except under the stimulus of
extreme necessity."[16] Community spirit abounds in the Japanese
village and most village events are supported by all households. A
water-rights dispute may well develop into a village-wide issue since
such problems are considered village problems—a result of the community consciousness created in the parent-child or master-servant
relationship.

A comparison of attitudes toward cooperation in farming likewise indicates that Japanese farmers are more cooperative than
their neighbors. Although some degree of cooperative exchange of
beast and human labor exists in China, such participation involves
only a few households. In general, cooperation is difficult in marginal intensive farming, but Japanese class interrelationships work
to encourage cooperative agricultural endeavors. The *kumi*, a
grouping of some ten households, which originated from the Tokugawa five-man system (*goningumi seido*) is also a more cooperative
system than the Chinese *pao-chia* system of ten households. Other
social groups in the Chinese village, too, appear less cooperative
than their Japanese counterparts.

---

[15] In China, when several small villages are united into an administrative
village unit, each village usually retains its autonomy. In this sense the Chinese
village appears rigid and closed in comparison with the Japanese village where
quite a few administrative functions have been transferred to the municipal
office; but since this problem must be considered in connection with national
administration, a mechanical comparison of the two should be avoided.

[16] G. Jamieson, *Chinese Family and Commercial Law*, Shanghai: Kelly and Walsh,
Ltd., 1921, p. 72.

VI. DIFFERENCES OF FAMILISM

Farming villages in both countries are composed of family-owned and operated parcels of land. The family, not the individual, is the component unit of the village and is the basis of all aspects of village life. Accordingly, basic family differences may explain the dissimilarities we have observed.[17]

The Chinese family emphasizes the principle of generation relationships and property equality, while in Japan lineal descent is emphasized. Herein lie the differences found in the family and clan structure as well as in the village organization. The Chinese rule of equal sharing prevents the maintenance of family status, and the status changes from generation to generation. As a result, the village power center shifts, the leaders' authority wanes, and no village-wide domination or status subordination develops. Occasionally, the local Chinese gentry can perpetuate its status in spite of property division, but no status relationship conducive to a development of traditional authority arises. In Japan, lineally determined familism permeates the entire village structure; the main, or parent, house can easily perpetuate itself through the family inheritance system, and thereby acquire traditional authority. The family, clan, and village function together and promote unity. Thus, in Japanese rural society, the main-branch family, parent-child, or master-servant relationship influences in some degree all aspects of village social life.

The traditional Japanese family system maintains relationships on a feudal basis: the main-branch house or parent-child relationship represents a lord-vassal status association and, therefore, Japanese familism may be designated a feudalistic familism. This type of feudal aristocracy could not be maintained in China, as Jamieson wrote, "by the levelling influence of the law of succession under which the splitting up of family properties sooner or later becomes inevitable.[18] The Chinese village lacks the atmosphere associated

---

[17] Because of the unique character of the family in China, there is a gap between the family and village. To be sure, a kind of familism peculiar to China is found on the village level. With this interpretation, Wagner's use of the term "Dorf-Familie" is understandable. W. Wagner, *Die Chinesische Landwirtschaft,* Berlin: Paul Parey, 1926, S. 174.

[18] Jamieson, *op. cit.,* p. 74.

with the parent-child, master-servant relationship common to Japan, and Chinese familism is not feudalistic.

Apparently, the lack of a prolonged feudal experience explains China's non-feudal family; and if it does, one needs to examine why a feudal system developed in Japan and not in China. An analysis of the physical, social, economic, and political conditions necessary to answer such a question is not only beyond the author's capacity but also beyond the scope of this study. Nevertheless, we cannot understand the differences in the cultures of China and Japan without exploring the question of feudalism in the two countries.

2. CHANGE AND STAGNATION IN THE INDIAN VILLAGE

I. The Modernization of India and the Significance of Village Studies

The constitution promulgated after Indian independence negated the social distinctions observed among members of the different castes and, in particular, announced that it would put an end to untouchability—preconditions for the modernization of India.

However, although it has been abolished by law, social discrimination on the basis of caste still survives. The acceptance of the principle that "all men are essentially equal" is an indispensable condition for the establishment of a modern society, but this principle is not in operation in Indian society, for distinctions of status based on birth are still to be found. It seems likely that, so long as the caste society exists in India, the development of India's economy will be impeded and the country will be unable to make steady economic growth. A society of the kind required by a modern economy is completely incompatible with the caste system.

Social discrimination on the basis of caste (and particularly discrimination against the scheduled castes—aboriginal peoples and untouchables) is more evident in the rural areas than in urbanized cities and towns. The Indian village is still as much a caste society as ever, a strong indication that India as a whole is still a caste society, for the overwhelming majority of Indians live in agricultural villages. In spite of the fact that India is one of the more industrially advanced countries in Asia, a large proportion of her population is engaged in agriculture and a large proportion of her production is agricultural products. The modernization of Indian agriculture and the Indian village are, therefore, indispensable conditions for the future development of the Indian economy, but

This essay, with a few minor changes, was originally published in *The Developing Economies*, Vol. II, No. 2, June 1964.

the caste system is an important factor impeding the development of Indian agriculture toward modernization.

Apart from its practical significance, an examination of the social structure of the Indian village with reference to the caste system is a subject of great academic interest; a number of surveys and studies dealing with this question have been produced by sociologists and social anthropologists. Not a few of these are notable contributions to knowledge. However, in the majority of these surveys and studies we cannot discern any pressure for the abolition of the caste system nor any guidance for the modernization of the Indian village. These studies give detailed descriptions of the social realities of the agricultural village, but they do not attempt to determine the direction in which change is taking place in the village, nor do they discuss the measures which must be adopted in order to eliminate caste society. This is undoubtedly due to the fact that this question is a difficult matter in which forecasts can scarcely be made, but it is also due to the fact that these sociologists and social anthropologists use a methodology which ignores "the economic approach."

In contrast to such studies, the surveys and studies which have been written from the point of view of the science of economics do not attach much importance to the caste system and related social factors. "Agro-economic research" is intensively pursued in India, and in this field also some excellent pieces of work have been produced, but the majority of these studies do not attempt, in any satisfactory way, to arrive at a synthesis of the economic structure and the social structure. The question of the relation of social and economic factors is of greater importance when we are dealing with people living in a pre-modern society separated in time from the *homo economicus* of the economists than when we are dealing with people in modern societies. More importance must, therefore, be attached to a sociological approach in such studies, and a sociological element must be incorporated in the economic interpretation of the subject matter.

Thus, in future studies of the subject, the sociologist and the economist must relate to each other and supplement each other. As R. Mukherjee[1] has pointed out, "The lack of a balanced view of

[1] R. Mukherjee, "On Village Studies in India," *Indian Journal of Scientific Research*, Vol. IV, No. 2, Dept. of Post-Graduate Studies in Sociology, J. V. College, Baraut U. P., 1963.

the dynamics of rural society" has been noticeable in studies of the subject. The tasks facing students of Indian modernization, therefore, are to take account of the imbalance, integrate sociological analysis and economic analysis, and determine the ways by which the modernization of Indian rural society may be accomplished.

It is from this point of view that we propose to discuss the topic of change and stagnation in Indian village society, concentrating our attention on the caste system. Because of the present circumstances of interdisciplinary studies and because of the writer's imperfect acquaintance with the subject, the following statement must necessarily be in the nature of an essay. In spite of these limitations, however, we think that such an essay may serve some useful purpose, if only because it will provide some degree of orientation for future studies.

II. THE TRADITIONAL STRUCTURE OF THE INDIAN VILLAGE

Before we address ourselves to the tasks of discovering the social changes which have taken place in the Indian village and of considering the direction in which these changes tend, we must first give some account of the traditional social structure of the village. Studies of the Indian village began in the early years of British colonial rule and arose out of the necessities of fiscal administration. It was inevitable that in the context of these studies the Indian village with its traditional social order should appear to the British writers as a "completely self-sufficient, isolated republic." Their studies of "the village community" were concerned with the self-sufficient socio-economic structure of the village, systems of communal landownership and collective responsibility in the payment of taxes, and the organs of village self-government which supervised these social mechanisms. The conception of the Indian village which was built up from the study of these aspects of rural society was that of an occluded communal social organism.

The Indian village may certainly be regarded as having maintained a traditional order of society and as having constituted an isolated universe in the period before the establishment of British rule. We may say with M. N. Srinivas that this isolation was a product of such "factors" as "the absence of roads," the "prevalence of widespread political instability," and the fact that "very little money circulated in the rural areas."[2] Of necessity, this state of society underwent some change under British rule. However, the essential nature of British colonial rule was such that it delayed the modernization of India, barred the way to industrialization, and did not lead to the break-up of the self-sufficient economy of the village.[3]

Of course, as B. Singh says, the idea that the Indian village was isolated and self-sufficient is a mixture of myth and reality.[4] M. N. Srinivas and many other writers have pointed out[5] that, although little currency was in circulation, a certain number of itinerant merchants roamed the country and weekly markets had been long-established. As we shall show, the self-sufficient division of labor in the village was indeed supported by the caste system, but members of every caste whose occupation concerned a daily necessity were not always present in every village. This was especially so in north India, where caste endogamy and village exogamy combined to draw the villagers into social relations which transcended the individual village. We need not add that caste *panchayat*s were organized which united caste members living in neighboring villages.

Further, although it is the practice to speak of "the village community," it is not true that the village was a communistic community in which all the villagers shared equally in the ownership of the land. No community of the kind which is characteristic of the idyllic classless society of primitive communism has been found in the caste society of the Indian village. The communal ownership of land did not exist in all Indian villages, and even in those areas where it did occur, distinctions were made between individuals in regard to their enjoyment of communal rights, and the institution of communal ownership was in practice much complicated by the caste hierarchy.

Nevertheless, the Indian village does possess certain characteristics in the understanding of which we can well employ the concept

[2] M. N. Srinivas, "The Industrialisation and Urbanisation of Rural Areas" in his *Caste in Modern India and Other Essays*, Bombay: Asia Publishing House, 1962, pp. 77–79.

[3] On this point, see R. Mukherjee, *The Dynamics of a Rural Society: A Study of the Economic Structure in Bengal Villages*, Berlin: Akademie-Verlag, 1957.

[4] B. Singh, *Next Step in Village India: A Study of Land Reforms and Group Dynamics*, Bombay: Asia Publishing House, 1961, p. 1.

[5] Srinivas, *op. cit.*, pp. 77–78.

of "the village community." Further, these characteristics are still seen in the modern village community, even though the traditional structure of the village is in the process of dissolution.

The Internal Organization of the Village

During the period of British rule, there were some villages which were inhabited by members of only one caste, but by far the greater part of them were "multi-caste" villages. The village community was composed of an arrangement of these castes, one above the other in a hierarchy whose rankings were clearly apparent in the practices observed in regard to commensality.

It was the general rule for the different castes to live in different sections of the village. The first thing which one notices about Indian villages is that the better houses are usually located in the center of the village, while the ill-kept and roughly-constructed houses are built around them or are located on the circumference of the agglomeration or at a slight distance from it. One can always distinguish at least two residential areas at first glance—the group of houses occupied by the dominant caste and the group of houses occupied by members of the scheduled castes.[6] These residential areas are denoted by the word *thola*, to which the name of the caste living in the area is prefixed. The castes which are represented by only a few persons live in the residential area of a larger caste of approximately the same social standing. For example, the Brahmins usually live in the residential area of the dominant caste. At present there is some irregularity in the geographical distribution of the castes within the village and some mixture of dwelling places, but we may suppose that in the traditional village the distinctions in regard to caste residential areas were carefully observed.

The castes living in the different residential areas were arranged in a hierarchy which was clearly legitimate in the eyes of the villagers and was accepted by them as axiomatic. This ritual ranking, however, was at the same time related to the economic stratification of the village. The dominant caste was also the landowning caste, while the scheduled castes comprised the poorest section of the landless inhabitants of the village. If we divide the Indian castes into three main strata—the upper stratum containing the Brahmins and

[6] On the concept of the dominant caste, see M. N. Srinivas, "The Dominant Caste in Rampura," *American Anthropologist*, Vol. 61, No. 1, 1959.

landowning dominant castes, the middle stratum containing the
merchant and artisan castes, and the lower stratum containing the
aboriginal peoples and untouchables—we may say that the representatives of the upper stratum were landlords and rich peasants
while the lower stratum was composed of landless laborers and
tenant peasants. The artisan castes in the middle stratum lived in a
state of dependence (economic as well as social) on the castes in the
upper stratum.

The Jajmani System as a Traditional Economic System
As we have stated above, the castes lived in separate residential
areas in the Indian village and the villager's consciousness of belonging to a particular caste was strengthened by the social and
geographical implications of the contacts which he made in the
course of everyday life. It would consequently appear that the village was split up into a number of caste groups, but in fact the castes
were bound together by the *jajmani* system, the traditional occupational organization.[7]

During the period in which the Indian village was more or less
based on communal ownership of land, certain social relations were
established under which the dominant castes, who had considerable
rights over the communally owned land, assumed a sovereign role
in food production, mobilized the labor of the lower strata, and
had the artisan castes manufacture and deliver goods for their consumption as well as agricultural implements, and paid these artisans
in kind with food grains. This was the *jajmani* system. This form
of economic organization did not operate on the principle of an exchange of equal values but took the form of services performed by
the artisan castes and the untouchables for the benefit of the dominant castes, in return for which the upper castes gave them an assured livelihood by means of payments in kind. The payments in
kind made to artisans by the landowners, that is, by the sovereign
power in agricultural production, remained at a fixed level, but the
quantity of goods manufactured by the artisans—for example, the
number of pots which a potter had to produce for his patron—was
not fixed but was dependent on the requirements of the patron. In
the case of the blacksmiths, too, there was no limit to the number of

[7] For a field survey of the *jajmani* system, see O. Lewis, *Village Life in Northern
India: Studies in a Delhi Village*, Urbana: University of Illinois Press, 1958.

occasions on which a peasant patron could command the services of the blacksmith for the repair of his agricultural implements. When there were two or more households of potters in the village, the patrons were divided into two groups. The amount of the annual payment in kind was not determined by negotiation between individual patrons and clients ('client' being used in the Roman sense) but was laid down by the caste *panchayats* of the persons in question, these decisions later receiving the approval of the village. Similar arrangements were made in the exchange of services between the artisan castes. Among the castes of the lower stratum of society, certain persons were granted an assured livelihood by the village. The sweepers, who were allowed to beg the leavings of food from the members of the upper castes, are one example. Their services at marriage ceremonies and funerals were rewarded by fixed payments. The same arrangement was made in remunerating the Brahmins for their officiation at religious ceremonies.[8]

The caste system, associated with certain traditional hereditary occupations, was maintained by the economic power of the landowners, that is, by the agricultural producers. Agriculture was not an occupation restricted to any particular caste, but in general it was the main occupation of the dominant castes, and they were the sovereign power in the economy of the villages. In these circumstances, agricultural production was never organized as a means of acquiring profit for re-investment and an expansion of the scale of production but was used to maintain the traditional mode of living in the village.

The Hereditary Structure of Village Self-Government

The institutions of village government which operated under this economic system were run by the dominant castes. The traditional power structure in village government was headed by a hereditary headman who was a member of the dominant caste. In many cases, members of certain families in the dominant caste were recognized as being eligible for the office of headman, and this eligibility was hereditary.

[8] The payments in kind made to the artisan castes are of a different character from the donations given to the Brahmins. See A. C. Mayer, *Caste and Kinship in Central India: A Village and its Region*, London: Routledge and Kegan Paul, 1960, pp. 63 ff, in which this question is discussed with reference to the two categories *Kamin* and *Mangat*.

The headman had to assume responsibility on behalf of the ruling power for tax collection and the maintenance of order, and thus received recognition as the headman of the village from the external political power. He collected the land tax with the co-operation of the *patwari*, who compiled the land register and calculated the taxes, and the *chaukidars*, who served tax notifications and demands. The *patwari* may be described as the village accountant; most of them were members of the Brahmin caste. In contrast, the *chaukidars*, who may be regarded as village policemen, were usually recruited from the scheduled castes. With the exception of serious offences, the headman had the power to inflict punishment on the villagers in the cause of maintaining law and order in the village. He was also, of course, the principal mediator in disputes among the villagers. Disputes within a single caste were settled by the caste *panchayats*, but disputes which the caste *panchayats* found themselves unable to settle, as well as disputes between castes, were submitted to the mediation of the headman. The headman also presided at many of the religious festivals celebrated in the village.

The headman's rule over the village was not a dictatorship. His position was strengthened by the support of the dominant caste, and behind his administrative power were influential members of the village community who, like himself, were members of the leading castes. Between the headman and the villagers were the caste leaders, that is to say, the leaders in the different residential areas of the village. We may be justified in supposing that at this period the actual operation of village government was in the hands of an informal assembly of elders composed of these leaders and dominated by the influential members of the dominant caste.

In concrete terms, this traditional power-structure differed in the *zamindari*-type villages and the *ryotwari*-type villages. There were also differences between villages in the areas which came under direct British rule and those in the areas in which the princely states retained their independence. In spite of these differences, however, we may say that, up to the beginning of the present century, the village was allowed a comparatively high degree of autonomy under the system of government we have described and that the economy of the village was largely self-sufficient.

III. Socio-Economic Changes in the Agricultural Village

The traditional socio-economic structure of the Indian village underwent gradual changes during the period of British rule. These changes became all the more marked after Indian independence. In particular, since the beginning of the twentieth century, the handicrafts which were maintained by the *jajmani* system have to disappear under the influence of modern industry. Further, the institutional changes in political administration which occurred after independence have had a strong impact on the traditional power structure of the village. No more than any other social organism could the Indian village—so typical of stagnant Oriental society—be spared the trials of modernization.

Economic Change and Traditional Occupations

The social changes in the village were brought about, first and foremost, by economic factors. Although it is true that imperialist colonial rule barred the way to industrialization, the economy of the Indian village could not remain completely unchanged as the times advanced. Economic development led to the penetration of money economy into the village, and the villagers came to regard a certain level of monetary income as a necessity. The villagers began to acquire some of the manufactured products of modern industry and modern industrial production could not but have some effect on the traditional occupational structure of the village. Some of the hereditary occupations associated with the caste system became unable to maintain themselves, and even where the traditional occupational system was not brought to complete dissolution, many of the traditional occupations required fewer workers than before. We may cite as an example, the case of the carpenters who had made ox-carts but who found themselves unable to compete with the vehicle-building works in the towns. When the carpenters living in a village were employed only in repair work, one carpenter could do the work formerly done by three. The same situation obtained in the case of the blacksmiths. When textile mills were established, the village weavers found that there was no work for them to do and they were obliged to abandon their traditional occupation.

Economic development also led to the appearance of new occupations. As the economy developed, even members of the castes whose principal occupation was agriculture were led to open shops in the villages and to act as dealers in various commodities. In areas near the cities there was an increase in the number of commuting factory and transport workers. In such villages, members of every caste began to live in closer relation with the cities, and changes were liable to occur in the socio-economic structure.[9] Even in villages some distance from the cities the Chamars in the lowest stratum of village society found that they could no longer make a living by preparing hides, and the weavers, having lost their traditional occupation and forced to find some other means of livelihood, became milkmen or left the village for temporary work in brick factories.

On the other side of the coin, these changes have also resulted in people who have lost their traditional occupations shifting to farming. The monopoly of land held by the dominant castes (the landowners and organizers of agricultural production) has been broken, and more and more people in the artisan castes and even in the scheduled castes own land and farm as their principal occupation. A discrepancy has appeared between the traditional hereditary occupations of the various castes and their actual occupations, and where this discrepancy has reached large proportions, the *jajmani* system itself has broken down. When this happens, the annual payments in kind which were intended to assure the livelihood of the workers under the *jajmani* system assume the form of remuneration paid in exchange for labor. Fixed payments in kind are then found only among a certain section of the richer peasantry, and cash payments become general. These developments have wrought great changes in the hitherto self-sufficient Indian village.

The Influence of the New Panchayat System
The second kind of change which has taken place in the Indian village lies in the realm of political administration. The British colonial administration made some impact on the village through the tax collection system, but if the taxes were paid, the colonial authorities did not actively interfere in village government. About 1920 attempts were made to establish a *panchayat* system, but this institution did not negate the existing village power structure. How-

[9] On this point, see T. S. Epstein, *Economic Development and Social Change in South India*, Manchester: Manchester University Press, 1962.

ever, the New Panchayat System, put into effect by the Govern-ment after independence, was basically incompatible with the exist-ing forms of village government. The electoral constituencies and the number of members in the new *panchayat*s were determined by population. The *panchayat*s were elected, and seats were reserved for members representing women and the scheduled castes.

We may describe this change in local government as a change from the rule of tradition toward the rule of legitimacy. We may draw attention to the following important points in connection with the new institution.

First, the hereditary principle has been renounced, and the prin-ciple of electoral choice of leaders has been adopted. We cannot equate this change with the change from "ascribed status" to "achieved status" as S. C. Dube says,[10] but the use of the electoral method in the choice of leaders implies a change in the type of leader. The new institution has at least opened the way to the over-throw of the dominant caste's monopoly of the office of headman. Second, village administrative decisions must now be made by ma-jority vote and not unanimity among the *panchayat* members. For-merly, decisions had been made by the leaders of the dominant caste, and a compromise agreement was regarded as the unanimous decision of the whole meeting. It was difficult for any of the members to resist such decisions, but now that the voting procedure has been adopted, members can express their opposition. Third, the connec-tions between the *panchayat*s and the external political power have been strengthened, and the questions discussed in the village include an increasing number of matters which can not be settled within the administrative institutions of the village. Even under the old system of local government the village was not completely closed and iso-lated, but it was more independent than it is now, and it was easy to maintain the social order of the village unchanged. We may say with D. G. Mandelbaum, "The old councils were arbitrary, con-serving agencies whose prime function was to smooth over or settle village friction. The new *panchayat*s are supposed to be innovating, organising bodies working for changes rather than conserving soli-darity."[11] The *panchayat*'s business brings it into contact with the

[10] S. C. Dube, *Indian Village*, London: Routlege and Kegan Paul, 1955, p. 222
[11] D. G. Mandelbaum, "Social Organisation and Planned Culture Change in India," in M. N. Srinivas ed., *India's Villages*, Bombay: Asia Publishing House, 2nd Edition, 1960, p. 19.

higher administrative organs of the Government in such matters as community development programs, extension work, and the organizing of agricultural co-operative associations. When such activities are undertaken at the initiative of the higher organs of government, there are more chances for changes of leadership at the village level and for changes in the forms of decision-making.

Urbanization and the Weakening of Social Unity

The progress in urbanization which has recently taken place is connected with changes in the structure of the economy and has led to changes in the social attitudes and value systems of the inhabitants of the villages. The deeply-rooted Hindu religious faith is still found in the villages in the form of religious celebrations or the rituals associated with them, and these practices are maintained in the traditional manner. However, even the religious celebrations no longer play as important a part in the life of the village as they once did. Again, with the progress of urbanization, the caste system, permeated as it is with the Hindu view of the world, has become less strict in its social distinctions. The Government has repudiated caste discrimination in the constitution, and it does not allow the traditional commensality rules to be observed at public functions in the villages or schools. Over a long period this will probably have a considerable effect. Such changes have also imbued the hitherto oppressed lower and middle castes with the desire to improve their social position. This desire is augmented by the increasing gap between the socio-economic stratification and the ritual rankings of the castes. As M. N. Srinivas says, even today "it is considered proper to follow one's traditional occupation," but "this view does not obtain among many of the younger people who have been to school and who are urban in their outlook."[12]

We may thus say that in the modern Indian village both village loyalty, the vertical ties centered chiefly on the dominant caste, and caste loyalty, the horizontal links which transcend the village and join members of a caste, have been weakened. M. N. Srinivas, who regards caste loyalty more important than village loyalty sees the village as the social unit which today commands the loyalty of

[12] M. N. Srinivas, "The Social Structure of a Mysore Village," in his *India's Villages*, Bombay: Asia Publishing House, 1960, p. 29.

all the villagers, regardless of caste.[13] D. Pocock and L. Dumont think that caste is fundamental,[14] but that the cohesion of the castes is now weaker than before. In recent studies of the Indian village, attention has been paid not only to the village itself but also to problems in the surrounding region and some emphasis has been placed on the castes' wide horizontal connections. In fact, however, this is not necessarily the case; what we must not forget in this connection is that the village is no longer a small self-sufficient cosmos. That is to say, the social changes which have taken place in the village are of such a character that they require some extension of the scope of village surveys and an examination of the question of the weakening unity of the castes and of the village community.

IV. SOCIAL STAGNATION AND THE LIMITS OF SOCIAL CHANGE

As we have noted, several aspects of Indian rural society have passed through processes of change. However, if we suppose that these social changes have progressed to a marked degree, this will be a more grievous error than the mistaken emphasis which is sometimes placed on the static and unchanging nature of the Indian village. At the Decennial Celebration Symposium of the Indian Sociological Society, at which the subject of discussion was of "The Nature and Extent of Social Change in India," one of the participants reporting on the internal condition of the village community could say no more than, "The social facet of Indian rural society is changing, but exceedingly slowly."[15] On a small scale, the Indian village has indeed changed, but in large scale terms we must acknowledge that absence of change predominates.

The reason for this situation is that, in spite of the changes which have occurred in certain aspects of village society, the caste hierarchy in the village is still generally in correlation with the economic stratification of rural society based on the ownership of land. The

[13] M. N. Srinivas, "The Social System of a Mysore Village," in M. Marroit (ed.), *Village India: Studies in the Little Community*, Chicago: The University of Chicago Press, 1955, pp. 34–35.

[14] L. Dumon and D. Pocock, "Village Studies" in their *Contributions to Indian Sociology*, No. 1, 1957, p. 29.

[15] J. F. Bulsara, "Nature and Extent of Social Change in Rural Society," *Sociological Bulletin*, Bombay: Indian Sociological Society, Vol. XI, Nos. 1 and 2, 1962, p. 169.

members of the dominant castes still own more land than the members of the other castes.

Sanscritisation and De-Sanscritisation

The present situation, therefore, is that although the foundations of the caste system have been shaken, the system has not yet collapsed. The status of the Brahmins, who formerly stood at the summit of the hierarchy of ritual caste ranks, has shown a tendency to decline in most of the villages. The Brahmins, in their capacity as priests, do indeed hold the highest position in society from the point of view of ritual, but as far as the daily life of the village is concerned, they are in a state of parasitic dependence on the dominant castes. The authority of the officials in the lowest ranks of the tax collection system has also declined, and the Brahmins employed in these offices are no longer highly regarded. Yet, in spite of these factors, the Brahminical way of life continues to exert a binding force in the village, and it is endowed with great value in the minds of the villagers. Consequently, when a disparity appears between the ritual rankings of the castes and the socio-economic rankings of their members, a movement to improve the status of the caste as a social group appears among the lower and middle castes. In practice this means that efforts are made to raise the status of the caste by acquiring the Brahminical value system and the way of life characteristic of the upper castes. This is the social process to which M. N. Srinivas has given the name "sanscritisation."[16] It may also be described as a reactionary movement back to caste-ism.

In contrast to this movement among the middle and lower castes, the general tendency among the upper castes has been to attach less value to the superiority of the caste and to become more westernized than the members of the lower castes. In particular, members of the dominant caste who have received an urban education have become more and more secularized and do not feel themselves so strongly bound by the Brahminical way of life as do the members

---

[16] M. N. Srinivas, "A Note on Sanscritisation and Westernisation," in *Caste in Modern India*, pp. 42–62. In a passage written on the occasion of the inclusion of this paper in the above work, the author puts forward the opinion that the concept of sanscritisation is complex and heterogeneous, that it is more of a hindrance than a help in making sociological analyses, and that it is better not to use it.

of the castes in the middle and lower strata who aspire to approximate the upper stratum of society. We may follow D. N. Majumdar in calling this process "deritualisation" or "de-sanscritisation."[17] This process is a counter-movement to the sanscritisation process of the middle and lower castes.

If both these processes proceed at a rapid rate, the natural result should be a lessening of caste differences. In fact, however, the dividing walls of caste are scarcely broken. The sanscritisation process does not in itself negate the caste hierarchy, and the aspirations of the middle and lower strata must be directed toward an improvement of the status of their castes as social groups—a difficult achievement. It is very difficult for all the members of a caste to improve their social and economic position and to raise the ritual status of their caste. Of the two processes, the de-sanscritisation process has the better chance of making headway. As Majumdar says, "The process of acculturation in India has been more a process of desanscritisation (or deritualisation) than that of sanscritisation."[18] Even so, this process is not very much in evidence in the agricultural villages. The caste hierarchy still exists and imposes limits on those forms of social change connected with the caste system.

The Difficulty of Solving the Problems of Untouchability and Poverty
In this connection we must point out that although the gap between the castes of the upper stratum and those of the middle stratum may have narrowed, it seems probable that the gulf separating the main body of castes from the scheduled castes will continue to exist. We recognize that the scheduled castes can now send representatives to the *panchayats*, but they are members only in name, and their voice carries little weight in the deliberations of these bodies. Again, they can make provision for the future by sending their children to school just like members of other castes, but there are many among the scheduled castes who do not have the economic resources to allow their children to go to school. The scheduled castes' economic status is altogether too low to erase untouchability, and until it is eradicated, the middle castes will have feelings of superiority toward the untouchables and will be

[17] D. N. Majumdar, *Caste and Communication in an Indian Village*, Bombay: Asia Publishing House, 1958, pp. 334–336.
[18] *Ibid.*, p. 336.

unable to put aside their caste-ism. Although they may aspire to raise the status of their castes in relation to those of the upper stratum, the middle castes will make no attempt to break down the caste system itself. Furthermore, while we acknowledge that it is among the untouchables themselves—among the people who have been oppressed by the caste system and have suffered under it—that we must look for those who will come forward to call for the abolition of the caste system, the untouchables are so poor that they cannot undertake such a reform of society. They are so driven by the necessities of self-preservation that thoughts of social revolution have no chance to arise. The poverty of the scheduled castes imposes limits on the social changes which can take place in the Indian agricultural village and is responsible for the economic stagnation which characterizes the village.

We would advocate the democratization of the village economy as a first step toward the alleviation of poverty. If land were given to the poor landless villagers, their economic standing would improve, but this is an unrealized hope. Land reform has been a great pillar of national policy in post-independence India. Each of the states undertook land reform in its own territory, but their measures were half-hearted. Not only was the ceiling of landholding very high, but men who held land in excess of the ceiling could retain it by distributing its nominal ownership among the members of their families. In any event, the population was too great in relation to the available area of agricultural land, and such half-hearted measures of land reform did not have much effect. Land reform did not rescue the scheduled castes from their plight, and they received practically no benefit from it.

Another means of saving the scheduled castes would be to press forward with industrialization and provide them with new places of work. However, when modern industry is imported from the advanced countries (as is the case in the less-advanced countries), the proportion of organic capital is generally high, and a particularly large amount of labor is not needed. The effect of such industrialization is rather to destroy the traditional occupations and drive the people employed in them into agriculture, thus increasing competition for the land. It also causes an increase in the number of persons employed as hired laborers, so that the livelihood of the scheduled castes is threatened. Those who cannot make a living with what they can earn as laborers in their own villages look for temporary work elsewhere, but their employment is not of a sufficiently stable nature to enable them to leave their villages and settle in towns near their places of work. Although they may take up temporary employment elsewhere, these people are obliged to keep their economic base in the village. Because of the hardships encountered in undertaking temporary work outside the village, some of these people have been compelled to acquire land, but this has only resulted in very small areas of land being acquired by a minority, and their social position as a whole has not been improved. No social change of an order sufficient to destroy the correlation between the caste hierarchy and the economic class structure can be expected from the employment of labor outside the village in temporary work. Even if these developments lead to some improvement in the economic condition of one or two members of this class, so long as the majority of the untouchable castes continue their despised traditional occupations and are dependent on the charity of the other village inhabitants, untouchability will not be eradicated.

The Characteristics of Agricultural Production

At present the form of agricultural organization in which the upper stratum employs labor of the middle and lower strata (especially the lower stratum) is still in general operation. Since the possibilities for non-agricultural employment outside the village are limited, there are a large number of agricultural laborers in the villages, and this surplus of labor results in the reduction of the laborers' wages to a minimum. The landowners, in a position to exploit this cheap labor, are devoid of any positive attitude toward the improvement of agricultural production. Their livelihood is assured by the present relations of production, and they feel no need to be enterprising in introducing new forms of agricultural technology. They can get an ample income without buying better agricultural implements or introducing more efficient methods of cultivation. Agricultural production is thus carried on under the direction of a peasantry which despises manual labor and has no intention of changing the traditional agricultural practices, and its economic organization goes no further than simple reproduction, for it is unthinkable that it should develop in the direction of investment in the expansion of the scale of production.[19] The idea of raising production, increasing incomes, and going forward to develop agriculture in an enterprising manner is completely foreign to them.

It is, of course, not true that absolutely none of the landlords wants to improve agricultural production. However, when only one or two of them have a progressive orientation, any new forms of technology which they may introduce will not be readily adopted on other village holdings if the economy of the village as a whole is static. Again, it is not true that Indian peasants do not want to increase their incomes, but even when they succeed in earning an income in excess of their immediate needs, they show no inclination to reinvest it. They accumulate savings to defray exorbitant wedding expenses or to rebuild or extend their living quarters. Further, although they will spend money in the purchase of status symbols, they will not buy new and improved agricultural implements.

In order to bring about some change in this situation, the Indian government has been pressing on with community development programs and the national extension service. However, these measures have benefited only the rich peasants of the upper stratum; most writers think they have accelerated the tendency to social stratification, and some are of the opinion that they have not only been of no use but have been positively harmful.[20] Great hopes were placed in the village *panchayats* as a means of pushing forward the development programs, but the financial resources at the disposal of the *panchayats* have been altogether too meager to permit them to come up to expectation.[21] The money invested in Indian agriculture under the successive Five-Year Plans has amounted to no inconsiderable sum, but it is no exaggeration to say that these funds, dispersed over so vast a country as India, have been barely sufficient to equip the agricultural base. No breakthrough has yet occurred in the stagnation which characterizes the Indian village.

[19] S. P. Bose, "Peasant Values and Innovation in India," *The American Journal of Sociology*, Chicago: The University of Chicago Press, Vol. LXVII, No. 5, 1962.

[20] A. R. Desai, "Community Development Projects—A Sociological Analysis," in his *Rural Sociology in India*, Bombay: The Indian Society of Agricultural Economics, 3rd Edition, 1961, p. 560.

[21] For a first-hand description of the financial situation of the village *panchayat*, see Part II, Chapter 2, "Social Organization in Indian Villages."

V. Towards the Modernization of Village Society

The Indian village's road to modernization is beset by many difficulties. In opening up this difficult road, India, like many of the
developing countries, has sought a solution in industrialization.
Whether this solution has been successful is by no means indisput-
able because modern industry does not absorb a large amount of
surplus population from the villages. At the same time, efforts are
being made to encourage cottage industry as well as modern industry, but there is no sign that cottage industry will be able to bring
about modernization in the Indian village.

Our conclusion is that the Indian village will not be modernized
unless some strong measures are taken in regard to agriculture itself.
Indian industrialization will not be able to expand and develop
unless there is an increase in the productivity of agriculture which
will make possible an accumulation of capital and an increase in
the purchasing power of the peasants.

The logical consequence of this situation is that first priority must
be given to the full equipping of the base of agricultural production.
This equipping of the productive base should commence with a
great leap forward in the improvement of irrigation facilities. Indian agriculture can exploit the climatic conditions of the country
with great profit, provided that water is made available. If matters
remain as they are at present, any attempt to encourage the adoption of new agricultural techniques will not be successful beyond
certain fixed limits. This may be inferred from the fact that the
Japanese type of rice cultivation has not been adopted in spite of
the Government's recommendations. Change in the productive
base increases the possibility for certain social changes. A large
amount of money will be required to equip the agricultural base,
and in order to acquire it, India should mobilize the surplus population of the villages on a large scale. She could use that labor
which is now idle because of the lack of employment opportunities,
and in doing so, overcome poverty and the overpopulation which
produces it. On this point India can well learn from the experience
of China.

Together with these measures, it will be necessary to inaugurate
a second land reform and to put into effect a radical land policy.
As we have noted, land is scarce in relation to population, so that

land reform in itself can have no great effect even if the landholding ceiling is drastically lowered. It is impossible to give land to all the peasants. What must be done is to alter radically the organization of the unit of management in agriculture and go forward to co-operative farming. At all events, some serious consideration must be given to the formulation of a policy which will make some drastic change in a system which enables landowners to abstain from labor. The modernization of Indian agriculture and the Indian village will never come about so long as the landowner class belonging to the dominant castes sits at ease, supported by the cheap labor of the lower strata. Nor will it be possible to destroy the caste system—the cancer of the Indian body politic.

However, the implementation of such drastic reforms in present-day India might result in the strengthening of the inefficient bu-reaucracy; in order to prevent matters taking this course, it will be necessary to strengthen the *panchayat* system. It will be necessary to strengthen the financial backing of the *panchayat*s, to give the villagers an increased interest in *panchayat* affairs, to nourish the villagers' consciousness of the significance of local government by getting them to engage in activities sponsored by the *panchayat*s, and to develop in them a growing capacity for democratic self-government. It need not be said that in the course of this process some increase in tension between the castes may occur, and a tem-porary retreat into caste-ism may result, but we must not be afraid of this. The nominal membership in the *panchayat*s enjoyed at present by the untouchables is devoid of meaning, and now is the time to go forward from caste antagonisms and caste conflicts to the task of overcoming caste itself.

Nevertheless, we cannot believe that the caste system will be easily eradicated. Modernization also requires the implementation of policies which will hasten the reformation of Hinduism. The chal-lenge to the Hindu value system cannot be avoided. No moderniza-tion can be expected in a country where cows are given more con-sideration than human beings. The power which resides in educa-tion must be applied in the systematic destruction of traditional attitudes. In the long run, the spread of education will bring about a transformation of society. On this point India will well learn from Japan. Japan's adoption of a thoroughgoing policy of compulsory education was one of the principal reasons for her rapid economic development, and more positive efforts should be made in this direction in India.

We need not say that such abstract policies as we have outlined are easy to express in words but difficult to realize in fact, and it is no simple undertaking to embody them in concrete administrative directives. Viewing the problem in the light of the social realities of the Indian village, we are obliged to say with M. N. Srinivas, "What kind of village community will come to exist in the future can only be a matter for speculation."[22] However, we feel that we should not be satisfied with the present situation, and we look forward to seeing among Indian scholars heightened interest in making scientific forecasts. The majority of Indian students of this subject were born in the higher castes, and although it cannot be denied that they have personal knowledge of the internal contradictions of the caste system and are themselves "de-sanscritized," we must frankly state that most of them have no strong desire to do away with the caste system. Freedom from the caste system is all too difficult a thing to achieve, but for this very reason is it not all the more necessary to tackle the problem seriously? Is it impolite for us to say this to our Indian friends? We do not think so.

[22] M. N. Srinivas, "The Social Structure of a Mysore Village," in his *India's Villages*, p. 35.

3. CHANGING JAPANESE RURAL SOCIETY

A) Changes in the Value System of Japanese Farmers

I. AGRICULTURE AND FARMERS IN JAPAN

Japan began to develop as a modern country with the Meiji Restoration of 1868. Therefore, Japan's capitalist economy has a history of less than 100 years. There are many factors associated with the country's rapid economic development, the relationship between agriculture and industrialization being one of the most important.

Agriculture was the only major industry in the nation 100 years ago. Japan had to depend upon agriculture in order to obtain necessary funds for the establishment of a modern administrative system and for industrialization after the Meiji Restoration. The Government received 80 per cent of its revenue from the land tax and it was as burdensome as the farm rents paid in kind during the feudal age. The Government, while imposing this heavy tax on agriculture, gave protection to the growing mining and manufacturing industries.

As is often observed in economically underdeveloped countries, modern industries did not easily absorb surplus agricultural labor. The number of farming households did not show any substantial decrease. The population of Japan continued to grow rapidly after the Meiji Restoration but the new industries were barely able to absorb the increase.

This essay was written for the First World Congress of Rural Sociology and originally published in *Sociologia Ruralis*, Vol. IV, No. 3/4, 1964.

The size of farms remained as small as in the feudal age, only one hectare—amazingly small compared with farms in Europe or America. The number of farming households also did not change appreciably from the initial 5,500,000 households.

The Government enforced a new land tax system in 1873 and ordered all farmers to pay the land tax in money instead of in kind. This caused a drastic change in the economic life of farmers for they were thus involved in a modern money economy quite different from the former self-supporting agrarian economy. The self-sufficient household economy of farm families collapsed under the ruthless force of modern business cycles. The number of tenant farmers increased while many owners lost their land. The farming class split into four strata: landlords, owner-farmers, owner-tenant farmers and tenant-farmers. The number of landlords was so few that each of the last three groups were almost one-third of the whole.

The relationship between landlords and tenant-farmers was characterized by high farm rents paid in kind. The right of continuous tilling for tenant-farmers was not stable. This unique relationship between landlords and tenant-farmers was the basic pattern of rural society in prewar Japan. The mining and manufacturing industries developed fast, but modernization of agriculture did not progress. As a matter of course, the agricultural productivity improved gradually through plant breeding and increased use of fertilizers. And it may be said that the social characteristics of farmers changed to some extent, corresponding to the socio-economic changes in their lives.

However, it is difficult to argue that Japanese agriculture changed basically. Paradoxically speaking, the fact that Japanese rural society as a whole did not undergo drastic change during the last century made a great contribution to the nation's industrialization. More specifically, the Japanese Government intentionally prevented farmers from becoming modern citizens in a modern society by means of particular indoctrinations. Farmers were thus forced to contribute to industrialization.

A money economy prevailed in rural society as Japan's capitalism developed. The backwardness of rural society became more conspicuous and various problems in agriculture came to the fore. An agricultural depression impoverished many farmers so that they could not maintain a subsistence income. Tenant-farmers began to organize into unions to bargain collectively with landlords. The union movement of tenant-farmers was active around 1920.

However, the nation's war structure in the period after the 1920's covered up socio-economic problems in agriculture and the farmer's movement was suppressed. The problems in Japanese agriculture became conspicuous again after World War II, and the post-war land reform program was undertaken to resolve the problem of land ownership. The land reform was executed throughout Japanese rural society, but it was not a revolution. The land reform succeeded in making owner-farmers but it did not enlarge the size of the farms. The productivity of agriculture has increased since the land reform, but it has been limited by the smallness of the farms. Post-war agriculture, however, has been influenced by those owner-farmers who obtained their farms through the land reform.

Of course, all of the Government's policies for farmers have changed since the war. Changes in the farmers' value system and goals have also been remarkable.

⌈Although the Japanese economy has attained an unusually fast growth rate in recent years due to the development of manufacturing industries, agriculture has lagged behind. Differences in income between manufacturing industries and agriculture have widened. The number of farmers seeking an additional source of income has increased greatly because incomes from agriculture are not enough to sustain life.⌋

A big increase has been observed in the flow of agricultural population into other industries. According to the latest statistics, the agricultural population has dropped to 25 per cent of the total population from the 40 per cent recorded ten years ago. Japanese agriculture has come to an important turning point in its history, a crucial time complicated by the fact that individual farmers do not have a guiding principle to orient their behavior.

II. FARMERS' VALUE SYSTEM IN PRE-WAR DAYS

Farmers' Personality Formation

The personality of Japanese farmers has been built up under the traditional institutions of family and village. The family-system was characterized by primogeniture in which the eldest son inherited the family property. The maintenance of family lineage was the highest of values in rural society.

All members of the family were to perform their individual functions under the control of the head of the family. The latter was empowered to restrict, if necessary, any personal desire of a family member for the "benefit" of the family as a whole.

The village was a unit community in Japanese rural society, and its most important characteristic was the cooperation of its members in rice production in the paddy fields. The village setting did not permit individual members of the community to freely engage in rice production. Furthermore, village as *Gemeinde* involved a landlord-tenant relationship which continued a rigid status hierarchy in Japanese rural society for many centuries. The village also provided different sets of behavioral norms for people of different social classes. These social norms were arranged so that each member could contribute, by following his status norms, to the maintenance of peace and order in the community under the authoritarian control of the landlords.

Within such a social setting, farmers developed unique personality attributes which ultimately served to maintain peace and order both in family and in community. Their personality thus constructed implied an attitude of acceptance of their status. They respected traditions unconditionally, and they were obedient to established authority. It was wise and safe for farmers to follow the traditional patterns of behavior. Whenever he had to make a decision about a problem, a farmer would consider the reactions of other members of his community. This was the guiding principle of his behavior.

It is easy to infer that the farmers were conservative. He had no motivation to initiate anything new. As a matter of course, this situation changed gradually as rural society became involved more deeply in capitalism. The pattern of family life changed and the old status hierarchy became unstable due to the structural transition of the economy. Some farmers began to try to raise their social status by accumulating wealth, which gave them an opportunity to satisfy the personal aspirations which had been restricted for reasons of "family benefit." Although there were some signs of change, the fundamental character of Japanese farmers, however, did not change until the end of World War II.

Attitude Toward Agricultural Production

It was not the practice of Japanese farmers to discriminate between farm management and household bookkeeping or between production and consumption. Family labor was regarded as free labor and farmers did not try to raise its productivity. It may be argued that Japanese farmers were too poor to purchase expensive farm machines, but more important is the fact that the value orientation of farmers was inconsistent with the idea of saving human labor through the use of machines. A high moral value was attached to daily toil, and farmers did not try to avoid hard labor. It was a philosophy among them.

Agriculture was not regarded as an enterprise in modern economic terms. The primary purpose of farming was to produce rice for family consumption rather than for sale on the market. Because the farmers believed that those who did not produce rice were not farmers in a real sense, they tried to grow rice even in areas where the land was not suited for rice production.

Rice production, it is well known, can be intensive so that the cultivation of a relatively small area of land can sustain a relatively large number of people. This is one of the traditional characteristics of oriental agriculture, but it has long hindered the development of agriculture as a modern enterprise. For instance, the cultivation of rice in paddy fields includes many conditions unfavorable for the use of modern farm machines: the use of machines in the tilling process has not been attempted, although extensive research in plant breeding and improvement of fertilizers has been undertaken.

Some Characteristics in the Consumption Pattern of Farmers

Cultural activity was irrelevant to those who spent twenty-four hours a day in toil and sleep. Indeed, "culture" and "cultivation" might have the same etymological origin, but the daily life of farmers was remote from what can be regarded a "cultural life." There is an old saying describing the life of farmers: "They go out to farm before daybreak and come home in moonlight." Even working such long hours, farmers had very low incomes. The Engel coefficient for farm households was as high as 51 in the period 1934–1936, against 35 for working class families in urban industrial areas. It was almost impossible for the average farm family to spare part of its income to raise its cultural standard.

The level of consumption among farmers was quite low. The philosophy of respecting hard labor and enduring low income was fortified by the ideas that consumption was a sin and thrift a virtue. We should note that respecting thrift was associated with accepting a difference in living standards because of a difference in social status. The tenant farmers did not begrudge or aspire to the landlords' higher standard of living.

However, the development of a modern economy began to disturb the traditional status hierarchy of rural society and motivated lower-class peasants to raise their status. Ambitious farmers began to practice thrift more seriously because the accumulation of wealth was the best available means for them to raise their status. Occasionally, the wealth accumulated by hard labor and thrift was wasted on ceremonial occasions: weddings, funerals, and community festivals. The money farmers wasted on wedding celebrations was unimaginably great in the face of the severe practice of thrift in their daily life. Such a conventional method of status demonstration was accepted as a normal matter of everyday life.

Physiocratic Ideology

As Japan's modern industrialization developed, most farmers became economically destitute. Primitive wealth accumulation—hard work and thrift—was of no use before the tremendous force of industrialism. Agricultural productivity was increased to some extent, but its improvement was slow in comparison with other industries, and made the backwardness of the farmer's life more conspicuous than ever.

Of course, farmers did begin to notice, though gradually, the disadvantages in their life. They then had to try to overcome these disadvantages or find psychological compensation from the fact that farming, although disadvantageous as a whole, had some benefits. Japanese farmers chose the latter; rather, they were forced to choose the latter. "Benefits" ascribed to conventional farm life came from an ideology that agriculture was the mainstay of the country. The physiocratic ideology had been advocated by the ruling class in the feudal period, and in modern Japan this ideology was widely advocated and widely interpreted by people representing different groups.

For example, industrialists advocated physiocracy in order to use farm families as a source of cheap labor. Some militarists used the ideology to protect the middle class farmers who were supplying the nation's armed forces with strong soldiers. Landlords were not the last to advocate the ideology because they feared a socialist-influenced farmers' movement. It is clear that all of these interpretations of physiocracy did not consider what would be beneficial for the farmers but were quite effective in giving farmers a certain psychological compensation for their depressed state.

The ideology of physiocracy indoctrinated farmers with the idea that agriculture was the most natural and wholesome of occupations and the key industry of the nation, and that urban industrialization was an important cause of moral degradation. At the same time, such indoctrination helped to keep agriculture the servant of modern industrial development. The political orientation of prewar Japan was imperialistic expansion, and it was thus unlikely that any effort could be made to develop agriculture at the expense of the modern mining and manufacturing industries.

Although diffusion of general education had virtually wiped out illiteracy in rural society, the deceptive ideology of physiocracy prevailed among literate farmers because their indoctrination was intensively and effectively promoted under the absolute authority of the emperor system.

III. Post-War Changes in Values and Goals of Farmers

Collapse of Physiocratic Ideology

Physiocracy's binding force was lost as a result of Japan's defeat in World War II. During the war, farmers were told that it was an honor to contribute to the "sacred war" through their farm work, but such an ideological indoctrination was found false when the wartime values collapsed. The ideological justification which had camouflaged the depressed state of agriculture was lost.

Even in prewar days, the development of modern industries provided many conditions for change in the value system of the farmers. These conditions, however, could not exercise their force upon the intensively indoctrinated farmers until the collapse of the old values. Of course, the land reform was one of the important factors in the subsequent changes in the farmers' value system.

The old landlord system was abolished by the land reform. All landlords became owner-farmers on a footing equal to those who had been their tenants. The old status hierarchy based on land ownership was affected. The binding force of the village was weakened following the collapse of the landlords' authoritarian control. The force of community traditions also became powerless. Various democratic provisions in the new Civil Code changed drastically the concept of the family among Japanese farmers. The Code curbed the privileges of the head of family and replaced the centuries-old system of primogeniture by establishing the legal right of equal succession to family property. (The equal succession to farm land is not actually practiced by many families, because the farms are too small to be subdivided.)

Changes in the Farmers' Attitudes toward Agriculture

Even before the war, Japanese farmers were aware that agriculture was a declining and unprofitable occupation, but they were forced to accept the *status quo* under the prevailing ideology of physiocracy. After the war they began to convert agriculture into a profitable enterprise. Having obtained their farms through the land reform, the farmers have been making greater effort to improve their productivity. In pre-war days, improving productivity might have raised the rent, but today an increase in production means an increase in income.

Another important change has resulted from the substitution of mechanization for family labor. Farmers now evaluate family labor economically. Hand-tractors, though small, have become an indispensable tool. Labor productivity has been greatly increased and the working hours of farmers have been shortened. Before the war, farmers were engaged in agriculture in order to support themselves, but today's agriculture is being operated to produce commodities, and farmers pursue agriculture as a business. Ten years ago farmers attached a special significance to their farms as valued property inherited from their ancestors, but a recent survey has indicated that the number of farmers who valued their land in terms of its productivity has increased considerably.

It is clear that the drastic changes in agricultural production are due to changes in the farmers' attitudes toward agriculture—attitudes that regard agriculture as a business.

Changing Attitude toward Daily Life

Under the traditional norms of rural society, farmers were forced to restrain the pursuit of secular ambitions. Consumption was regarded as a sin and any cultural aspiration was considered an unattainable luxury. Farmers, however, have started to pursue their aspirations openly since the war and defeat removed the traditional restraints, and this pursuit has accelerated farm production and motivated the farmers to further develop agriculture.

Associations have changed: those farmers who were previously tenants look upon their old landlords as their colleagues. Living standards have also changed. The collapse of traditional familism has encouraged farmers to take care of the "living members" of their families rather than their dead ancestors. They do not try to increase the family property by practising thrift and hard work; they do not want to give up their enjoyment of television to do so. To-day, more than 70 per cent of the agricultural households possess television sets; more than one-fourth use electric washing machines. The farmers have western-style suits for holiday outings; their wives regularly visit beauty shops like their counterparts in urban areas.

The diet of farmers has also changed. The variety of seasoning used in cooking has increased. Their housing has been improved: special emphasis has been put on the modern kitchen. Quite a few farm houses are now equipped with a modern water system.

Formerly farmers had few opportunities for recreation because rural society lacked the facilities. What they could enjoy were folk-dance parties in the Buddhist *bon* festival, festivals at the community shrine, and occasional visits of drama troupes. Since the war farmers have more actively pursued amusement. Eighty-five per cent of rural residents go to movie houses at least once a year, according to a survey. The young people often go to movie theaters in nearby towns. Sightseeing tours by bus are popular among rural people, both young and old.

The educational interests in rural society have increased greatly. Farmers long believed that education beyond primary school was useless, but the proportion of young boys and girls who attend a senior high school has increased rapidly. Adult education has also been encouraged. General adult education courses given at community centers and the activities of women extension workers, as a part of the agricultural extension service, are contributing much to the cultural development of rural residents.

Urbanization of Rural Society

As we have said, Japanese agriculture has become commercialized and farmers now try to get a larger income out of agriculture in order to satisfy their increased material desires; but the smallness of the farms remains the bottleneck in the development of agriculture as a modern enterprise. Even before the war many farmers were unable to maintain life on their income from agriculture. Farm households which did not have an additional source of income from supplementary employment were only 41 per cent of the total in 1941.

The farm households which did not have outside jobs increased to 50 per cent immediately after the war. Part of the increase was due to the destruction of industries during the war, but the proportion of farm households engaging in outside jobs has been increasing steadily since then because the level of consumption has risen faster than agricultural productivity. The total in 1955 was 65 per cent; in that year also as much as 27 per cent of the farm households were operating farms only as a source of additional income. The proportion of such households increased to 32 per cent in 1960 and recently exceeded 40 per cent. Those households which do not have any source of income other than agriculture are estimated as one-fifth of the total.

Farm families' supplementary employment covers a wide variety of occupations. Particularly since the war, the number of those who commute to industrial establishments or business offices in nearby cities has increased remarkably, and families in this category may not be regarded as farming households any more. It is estimated that only 40 per cent of today's Japanese agricultural households deserve to be called real farming families, 20 per cent receive equivalent incomes from agriculture and additional sources, and 30 per cent should be regarded as non-agricultural households. The remaining 10 per cent of the families are in financial difficulties because they lack male adult members.

Roughly speaking, farm households can be classified into two broad categories. The first includes those households operating farms on a commercial basis and producing crops as commodities.

The second consists of those operating farms only to produce rice and vegetables for family consumption, *i.e.*, subsistence farming. Families of the latter category, in most cases, are sending their members into urban industry. Those employed in good jobs are encouraged by the household because even if their wages are relatively low, the rice and vegetables produced by other members of the family are enough for family consumption.

Those rural people commuting to urban employment have daily contact with the value system of urban society. Thus, the traditional values of rural society are influenced by urban values. The prevalence of television in rural society is another important factor changing traditional values. Those farmers who are operating on a commercial basis are under pressure to modernize their farming to meet financial requirements arising from the adoption of an urban living standard.

Farmers usually depend upon agricultural cooperative associations to ship their products to profitable markets. Such shipments are undertaken collectively, and farmers are trained in a rational pattern of attitudes and behavior through these cooperative activities. Under such circumstances, the two groups of farmers we have classified can no longer operate on a single community basis because their interests are not identical. In other words, those operating farms on a commercial basis organize their own group for the pursuit of common goals. Their interests are becoming quite different from those of farm families employed in outside jobs. The old village community was expected to perform diversified functions to satisfy its members, but the community has begun to split into interest groups which perform different functions.

IV. OBSTACLES TO A COMPLETE CHANGE IN VALUES

In the preceding section evidence was presented that the value system of rural society has changed since the last war. There is a thesis that this change is an inevitable consequence of industrialization. As modern industries develop, the money economy prevails to control economic life in rural society and the general development of industrial society does not leave agriculture far behind. If this thesis is true, the value system of the Japanese farmers could have changed earlier; but it did not because the development of modern industries was promoted at the expense of agriculture.

It is also true that physiocratic ideology covered up conflicting problems in rural society and blocked the development of new values in the life of farmers and thus, since its collapse, the tempo of change has been rapid. However, because such rapid change cannot maintain a balance between such different values, there have been lags; for example, a farmer's familistic values cannot keep pace with a change in the attitude toward new farming techniques.

It may be argued that innovations in the rural value system have been retarded in recent years by a number of obstacles. The most important of these obstacles is undoubtedly the smallness of the farms. Japanese farm households are not given the necessary conditions to establish modern-sized farm operations. The young people in rural society who do not expect much from agriculture have been flowing into other industries, and most farm households have now found it difficult to retain successors for farm operations.

For a transformation of the value system of Japanese rural society, the following requirements will have to be fulfilled. A firm policy for the benefit of rural migrants to urban industries must be established; the number of farm households must be reduced substantially so that the size of individual farms can be larger than at present; and farmers must cooperate in collective farm management. In order to modernize Japanese agriculture, a large amount of money will have to be invested, even if such investment impedes the nation's total economic growth.

One can expect that rural values will be modernized and farmers will have established goals only when the modernization of agriculture is more completely carried out. In this respect, Japan's experience since the Meiji Restoration, and particularly since World War II, will be useful to developing countries. The development of modern industry is not the panacea which will modernize rural values. A rapid industrialization, rather, hinders the growth of agriculture and increases its problems. Agriculture has to be given favorable conditions for its own development.

This broad hypothesis will be applicable, in principle, to any society. The values and goals of farmers can be affected by the development of industries other than agriculture, but the development of a modern agriculture is a prerequisite for a balanced change in the farmer's value system. An agricultural development that keeps pace with other industries necessitates a firm policy to provide a new basis for agriculture.

B) Japanese Agriculture Today and Tomorrow

I. THE CHANGES OF RECENT YEARS

The post-war agricultural reforms marked the beginning of a new period of development for Japanese agriculture. With the dissolution of the landlord system which for so long had dominated agriculture, the number of owner-farmers increased greatly. They set to work with renewed vigor, and their productive capacity gradually expanded. Harvests of rice, the chief crop, increased steadily, and fruit and livestock farming underwent a remarkable expansion. Progress was also made in mechanized farming, although on the small scale characteristic of Japan.

TABLE 1.   Farm Households by Ownership Status (Percentage)*
Before and After the Land Reform

Year	Owner-Farmers	Owner-Tenants	Tenants
1946	32.8	38.4	28.7
1950	61.9	32.4	5.1
1960	75.2	21.6	2.9

* Some farmers have no land; hence the total is less than 100%

However, these developments were not enough to make everything smooth sailing in Japan's agricultural communities. Although the reforms undoubtedly helped democratize them, they did not solve the problems of agriculture as such. They were, literally, reforms, and not a reformation, much less a revolution. Although the agricultural land reforms transferred the ownership of land and created large numbers of new owner-farmers, they did not enlarge the farms. The petty farming—the excessively small size of the farms—which is the curse of Japanese agriculture, remained untouched. What is more, for several years after the war the agricultural communities had to support the large population which had

This essay was originally published in the *Japan Quarterly* Vol. XIII, No. 1, 1966 flowed in from the cities or Japan's former colonies; the number of farming households, which had remained around 5,500,000 since Meiji times, reached 6,200,000, and the average size of the farm shrank from a prewar one hectare to 0.8 hectare.

Thus despite the increased productivity and bigger crops, the excessively small scale of Japanese agriculture compared with that of other nations contributed as ever to work as a definitive limiting factor. Furthermore, although better harvests may have increased the farmers' gross income, the costs of fertilizers and chemicals also increased, and the expense of buying machinery came as a severe additional burden. Yet again, living standards among farmers, which in prewar times had been excessively low, increased year by year after the war. Most farmers found it impossible to maintain this new standard with their income from agriculture alone.

This state of affairs became still more marked in the course of the subsequent development of the Japanese economy as a whole. Industry, which had been utterly destroyed in the war, began a rapid recovery from around 1955 and showed a high rate of growth. The development of the manufacturing industry was especially remarkable and, with this as its focus, the scale of the Japanese economy as a whole has increased two-and-a-half times in the past ten years. Compared with this annual rate of growth of nearly 10 per cent for the whole economy, the figure of less than 4 per cent for agriculture, though an undoubted increase, is disappointing. As a result, agricultural income, which ten years ago accounted for close to 20 per cent of the gross national income, was shown in a recent white paper on agriculture to have dropped below the 10-per-cent mark. The importance of agriculture in the national economy has dropped sharply, and the gap between incomes in agriculture and other industries has been a constant topic of discussion for several years.

Besides this, the abnormal growth of industry and the widening income gap between agriculture and other industries has rapidly drained labor from the farming villages, which were already complaining of serious trouble in disposing of the second and third sons of families. Thus the factors tending to drive out population from the farming villages and those tending to draw it out combined forces. In 1955, the agricultural population still accounted for 40 per cent of the total working population, but by 1960 the figure had dropped below 30 per cent, and more recent (late 1963) statistics show that it has dropped to 26 per cent. By now, it is probably less than 25 per cent. The decrease has been especially serious during the past few years, assuming almost landslide proportions. Some 60 per cent of those who drift away from the farms—estimated recently to number nearly one million every year—are newly graduated from school. Fifteen years ago, more than 25 per cent of the new graduates were going into agriculture; five years ago the proportion was around 10 per cent, and by March 1964 it had reached an all-time low of less than 5 per cent. However, the drift of the agricultural population into industry did not always mean a decrease in the number of farming households. Recent statistics show that the figure, which still stood over six million households in 1960, has just begun to decline. It was about 5,800,000 at the end of 1963, and dropped to 5,665,000 at the 1965 census, which means that it has only just returned to roughly the prewar figure. In constrast, the agricultural population had already fallen below the prewar levels to 13.7 million in 1960 and dropped to 11.5 million in 1965.

The great imbalance between the rate of decrease in the agricultural population and the number of farming households means, ultimately, that although the younger male population tends to drift into industry the farms are still being run by the women and old folk. The sharp drop in the number of farmers has increased the proportion of old folk and women among them. Put in a different way, it means that Japanese agriculture is rapidly becoming a part-time occupation.

Even before the war, of course, farms were so small that at least one-half of all farm households had some secondary source of income. However, the increase in the number of households during the past ten years is not only different in character but is taking place at a rate which bespeaks a violent shift in the agricultural communities. The figure of 65 per cent for farms with secondary sources of income which was reached ten years ago had not shown any remarkable increase five years later in 1960, but the proportion of farmers with a "second-type" secondary occupation (*i.e.* where the secondary occupation is more important than farming) increased by as much as 5 per cent, so that full-time farmers, farmers with a "first-type" secondary occupation (*i.e.* where farming is still more important), and farmers with the second type of secondary occupation each accounted for approximately one-third of the total. The trend has since become still more pronounced, and the 1965 agricultural census showed that full-time farmers accounted for only 21 per cent, whereas the second type of part-time farmers accounted for 42 per cent. Full-time farmers have shifted to first-type secondary occupations, and the first-type secondary occupations to second-type secondary occupations. As a result of this trend, farmers' income from sources other than agriculture has come to exceed their income from agriculture itself. In other words, Japanese farmers today, viewed as a whole, have come to rely for more than half their income on sources other than agriculture. The Japanese farmer is barely half a farmer by now.

TABLE 2.
Farm Households: Full-Time and Part-Time

Year	Full-time farmer	Part-time farmer	
		First type	Second type
1955	50.0	28.4	21.6
1955	34.8	37.7	27.5
1960	34.3	33.6	32.1
1965	21.4	36.8	41.8

When the situation is viewed as a whole, this pronounced trend toward secondary occupations is creating regrettable conditions which will prohibit further increases in agricultural production. Admittedly, agricultural production is showing an increase of a kind. Indeed, some villages which have taken up fruit-growing and stock-raising are pursuing a course of "selective expansion" which has led to a remarkable development in production. Nevertheless, if still more farmers find secondary jobs and the number of farms producing only enough rice for their own consumption continues to increase, increases in agricultural production will almost certainly come to a halt. The more energy they devoted to their secondary occupations, the more the will to produce among farmers supplying their own rice needs will decline. With a decline in both the quantity and quality of labor, production costs will pile up and agriculture will become less and less profitable. The number of small power cultivators, roughly the equivalent of American garden tractors—in themselves a symbol of the uneconomical, Japanese-style mechanization of agriculture—has increased from 82,300 ten years ago to some 2,155,000 today, and this too can be taken as a reflection of the shortage of labor occasioned by the drift of the agricultural population to the towns and the tendency to find additional work.

II. Changes in the Agricultural Community

The increasing tendency for farmers to find outside jobs is a world-wide phenomenon; it is marked in America, and the European countries are no exception to the rule. In Japan, however, the trend is particularly rapid, and the changes taking place in the make-up of the agricultural community are correspondingly serious. In Japan, moreover, this rapid change is not accompanied by the appearance of any new road to reconstruction, and the old system and organization are having perforce to carry on as they stand, which poses still greater underlying questions.

In comparison with the prewar period, the farms have undergone a major transformation. It is not that a truly modern family life has emerged, nor has the old family system disappeared, yet there has been a marked decline in the specifically "feudal" aspects of farm life. One of the conditions for this has been the tendency for farmers to find other, non-agricultural work. Such work can be divided into three types: work involving wage labor on a permanent basis; migrant labor (involving work away from home during slack seasons) and day labor; and additional work undertaken on the farmer's own account. Recent nationwide statistics show that these three types account for 49 per cent, 29 per cent, and 22 per cent, respectively, of all side jobs. In each of the three cases, it is the old folk and women who have to shoulder the additional load of farm work at home. This admittedly has the effect of heightening the position of the women in the family but, at the same time, in most families where "the mistress is the farmer" the pressure of work has a deleterious effect on the women's health and a harmful effect, indirectly, on the children. Farms where the men commute to work daily are relatively fortunate. The really serious problems arise on the farms where the men leave home to work elsewhere. The high rate of economic growth has increased the range of jobs to which farmers may commute daily and—although many of these are little better than jobs as temporary hands—has at least increased the proportion of farmers who do their outside work for wages on a more or less stable basis. It has not, however, succeeded in providing adequate, lasting employment for all farmers who need additional work. The process of growth has seen an increase, in fact, in the number of farmers working away from home in the off-season, as day laborers, or in other such unstable side jobs. 1965 statistics showed, for instance, that the number of such farmers had reached 2,140,000, an increase of 860,000 or 67 per cent over the figure for 1960. Whereas the number of cases who were away from home for more than one but less than six months was about 200,000 in 1961, it had increased to about 300,000 by 1963; the figure is doubtless considerably higher by now and would be even larger if those farmers were included who were missed by the survey or who work away from home for more than six months each year. This leaving home to find work is a phenomenon common to all regions and districts where commuting to other work is impossible and it extends even to the comparatively large farms. The men who go away to work leave their families and embark on an unnatural life of separation from their wives in the hope of supporting their families or of finding a little happiness. In practice, the separation not infrequently leads to the destruction of family life. Even without this, leaves its scars on the man himself, as well as on his wife and children.

A further effect of this practice of finding outside jobs has been to complicate the structure of the village. The average agricultural settlement in Japan consists, statistically speaking, of 39 farming households and 25 non-farming households, a total of 64 in all. If the 39 farming households are broken down to show the proportions of those engaged exclusively in agriculture and those engaged in agriculture and other occupations, only eight are engaged full-time in agriculture while 14 are engaged in first-type part-time occupations and 17 in second-type part-time occupations. This suggests that the structure of the village as such may have begun to change, and that the unity of the small local community will be destroyed. Even the prewar agricultural communities were not made up of one uniform type of farm but had owner-tenant class distinctions and groupings of full-time and part-time farmers. The farming village of the past maintained an organization, with the landlord at its head, which regulated agricultural and social life in the village as a whole. Today, however, a split is developing between the full-time farmers who seek to live by increasing and diversifying agricultural production, and the part-time farmers who produce only enough rice for their own requirements, keep their land for retirement-security, and earn most of their income from their outside jobs. Thus it is difficult for a village to have a common sense of purpose even where agriculture is concerned. Moreover, there is an increase in the number of non-farming inhabitants who live in the villages solely because they cannot find homes in the towns where they work. The village, in short, has lost its character as a single, integrated community.

In the village of the past, the whole village participated in every aspect of social life. When a group was formed to carry out a particular function, every qualified inhabitant became a member, irrespective of his own inclinations. It was normal, too, for the village to deal with all kinds of expenses—whether for agriculture, civil engineering works, or festivals—as part of a single communal account. Every household, moreover, provided free labor for such village tasks as road upkeep and repair of the irrigation channels. This traditional arrangement is no longer appropriate to the village of today. Where village expenses are concerned, for example, agricultural association expenses have had to be put on a separate account, and the essential identity of the village and the association has been destroyed. The new heterogeneity of village members and the new diversity of their interests conflict with an integrated organization of village activities. For example, the custom whereby each household sends one of its members to participate in some village undertaking does not accord with the fact that households today do not always share a common interest in these undertakings. Moreover, the rapid drift of the younger men away from agriculture makes it difficult to find enough labor for a particular village undertaking. In some places there have not even been enough men to form a fire brigade, and the women have had to form a brigade. This trend is particularly marked in districts where the men emigrate to seek work, but it applies, with differences of degree, even in the villages where it is possible for the men to commute to their secondary occupations. The situation is particularly serious in forestry communities, where nothing is possible without communal labor. It sometimes happens that whole families will desert such a village because it no longer provides the means to maintain a new, higher standard of living; if the remaining households find it impossible to function as a village, in the end the village itself is disbanded and disappears. Yet while the villages of the past are breaking up, the old idea of the village as an integrated community is still deep-rooted. Loose though the bonds of loyalty which have always bound the village together may have become, they have not yet broken. The village retains, fundamentally, the same kind of organization that it had in the days when its inhabitants acted as an undifferentiated unit. The inhabitants find they can manage somehow even as things are, and village government carries on just because, in a sense, it is government by old people with a considerable degree of conservatism. There is, it is true, an increasingly pronounced tendency for the younger generations to work out arrangements more in accordance with the times where the practical functions of the village are concerned, but they make no attempt to carry out a reorganization of the village's system of government.

The third factor is the strengthening of the ties between the village and the outside world. Not only have its bonds with the town been tightened economically, in terms of production and consumption, but they are more closely connected in political administration as well. Farms producing commodities for sale have been expanding their connections with the markets, while those farms which produce only enough rice for their own consumption have been looking to the towns as sources of outside work. Moreover, the increase in the level of consumption has brought the towns as suppliers of consumer goods into closer contact with the village. The increasing number of farmers with outside jobs and the gradual urbanization of the farmer's life are increasingly interdependent factors. Nor should one forget, in the administrative sphere, the large number of towns and villages which have been amalgamated with the cities, doubling the number of cities and reducing to about 3,500 what was once a total of some 10,000 cities, towns, and villages.

What is more, the various villages and hamlets making up the agricultural communities have, as we have already seen, become more complex in their make-up so that an integrated community life based on identity of agricultural interests is no longer possible. Thus it happens that within a local self-governing unit, community of interest based on occupation or on class—*i.e.* disparity of wealth —comes to form horizontal bonds among the inhabitants which cut across the old village or hamlet loyalties, and these bonds have to be stressed if the tendency of local government to favor the towns is to be resisted. Yet the old loyalties, though weakened, are still alive even here. Even today when amalgamation has reduced the number of local assembly members and each village or hamlet can no longer send its own member to its city, town, or village assembly, the purely local interests of the district are still represented in the assembly; and although the members may not represent the hamlet or village explicitly, the impulse to vote for the local man is still deep-rooted. One factor that encourages this is that since Japanese local self-governing bodies have to run their affairs on economy lines, they continue to use the hamlet as a convenient subsidiary administrative unit. The link with the administration of city, town, and village reinforces the unity of the hamlet as an administrative unit and offers an inducement to the inhabitants to comply with the seemingly nonpartisan, abstract principle of local community of interest. When such community of interest becomes a principle influencing politics or administration, it serves to cover up class conflicts and—in villages as they are at present—occupational differences of interest, thus making difficult the rational administration of local government.

III. Political Moves Affecting the Agricultural Communities

We need not point out that under such circumstances the relative importance attached to agriculture in local administration gradually decreases. The proportion of farmer-members in local assemblies has decreased since so many villages, towns, and cities have amalgamated. In most cases the mayor has no connection with agriculture. Since amalgamation, the friendly village office has become impersonal and bureaucratic. And, as a result, assembly members from the farm districts have to serve as intermediaries between the villagers on the one hand and the impersonal mayors and bureaucratized local government organizations on the other.

This intermediary function gives them the status of local bosses, but they do not have the power of the assembly members elected from trade and industrial circles by the urban districts. Furthermore, in the present impoverished state of local finances, which tends to encourage assemblies to put money where it is most likely to bring in revenue, the funds voted for comparatively unrewarding agricultural administration are liable to be small. In short, the agricultural aspect of local administration is often neglected.

In many cities, towns, and villages, fortunately, this neglect is compensated by state subsidies to agriculture. Government policy toward agriculture is based upon the Fundamental Law of Agriculture, enacted in 1961. The preamble of this law states that "the duties springing from our concern for the public welfare, and necessary complements to the mission of agriculture and of the agriculturalists in our society are to ensure that those disadvantages resulting from the natural economic and social limitations of agriculture are corrected, to promote the democratization and rationalization of agriculture while respecting the free will and initiative of those engaged in it, and to ensure that the nation's farmers can enjoy a healthy and happy life not inferior to that of other members of the society." The purpose of the law is defined as being "to indicate clearly the new directions which agriculture must take and to establish policy objectives in regard to agriculture."

Under the new law the Government began its Agrarian Structure Improvement Program. It aimed to put Japanese agriculture —brought to a virtual impasse by the excessively small size of its farms—into better shape, and it was also motivated by the desire to make Japanese agriculture a better competitor in the international market. The Government's plan envisages that on a basis of 0.3-hectare rice fields, mechanically cultivated by tractors, farm productivity will increase and farmers' incomes will compete with incomes from industry.

The Government decided that work should be effected over a period of some ten years, beginning in 1961, in approximately 3,100 cities, towns, and villages, excluding areas expected to be affected by industrialization. It also planned to set up three-year pilot areas to serve as a guide. The maximum funds to be made available in ordinary areas totalled ¥110 million—¥90 million for subsidies and ¥20 million for government loans. In the pilot areas, where a particular district of a city, town, or village is due for intensive guidance and aid, the amounts are ¥60 million for subsidies and ¥15 million for loans. The sums might seem enormous but, in view of the ambitiousness of the goals, they are a small price to pay if they put Japanese agriculture on its feet. Nevertheless, it is not easy for individual farmers to find investment capital equivalent to half the sum of the subsidied projects and the whole sum of the projects financed by government loans, and it is difficult for them to pay back the debts incurred.

Thus the question is whether structural improvement in Japanese agriculture, even if successful, would mean an equivalent improvement in the condition of the farms themselves. Modern, mechanized agriculture would doubtless lead to high labor productivity, but an increase in productivity does not necessarily lead to increased profits for the farmer. Where a decrease in working hours per unit of land is not accompanied by a tangible increase in yields or by the chance to make additional outside income, the farmer is inevitably overwhelmed by the interest he owes on the capital he has invested. If this is to be prevented, there must be, first of all, a substantial decrease in the number of farms, but the Government has made no provision for this in the present plans. Nor has adequate consideration been given to whether modern, mechanized agriculture is really practicable in Japan. Nor has any detailed estimate been made of how many regions, in a country where barely half the farming villages lie on level land, are topographically suitable for mechanized agriculture.

One can only conclude that the Government's plans will not save the farms from the crisis afflicting them, except in a few favored areas. A white paper on agriculture published at the beginning of 1965 reports that the total number of areas (including the pilot areas) where the program has been put into effect is about 800 cities, towns, and villages, or about one-fourth of the number scheduled. There are grave doubts, however, as to how many of these areas are capable of real structural improvement. This does not mean that the measures devised to improve the structure of agriculture are in themselves wrong: the often-heard criticism that they would sacrifice the poorer farmers for the sake of the whole is far too oversimplified. No amount of cooperation among almost-landless, part-time farmers is going to raise Japanese agriculture to an international level. It is because the Structure Improvement Program contains no provisions for migration or occupational change that it is open to criticism as a "wiping out" operation; the structural improvement of agriculture remains as necessary as ever.

One of the most promising political steps which could be taken in connection with this prime necessity of encouraging the shift from the land is, obviously, regional development of industry. Here, too, policies were first advanced some ten years ago, but they have been attracting particular attention the past few years because of the desire of some local governing bodies to increase their sources of revenue by encouraging the building of factories. Since the adoption of the plan to double the national income, the encouragement of factory-building and regional development of industry have been central themes of both central and local government in Japan.

The talk of industrialization encouraged local leaders to believe that if they attracted factories to their localities, the resulting revenue from, for example, real estate tax would replenish the local coffers and in time benefit the local inhabitants as a whole, bringing prosperity to the area. With this in mind, city, town, and village authorities passed ordinances designed to attract industry—giving exemption from or reduction of business and real estate taxes, offering help in finding sites for factories, and promising to undertake water supply and road costs. They leaned over backwards to offer favored treatment to potential new firms, dreaming of the day when their districts would become industrial areas.

In most cases, unfortunately, the dreams were no more than that. So long as the present exclusive emphasis on industry prevails in development plans, regional development will be ineffective assistance to the farming areas, since it will not draw off labor from agriculture, encourage families to give up farming, or reduce the number of farms. Everything would be ideal, of course, if the development of industry of a type well matched to local conditions made it possible for a number of farm families to leave the farms, and the remaining farmers tackled the task of creating a new, healthier agriculture. In practice, even where new factories have been built and the region developed, the factories do not absorb as much of the agricultural population as expected. (The more technically advanced the firm the less laborers are needed—and the native, unskilled labor force is not qualified.) The building of factories may lead to the creation of new jobs, but these do not automatically offer complete security of livelihood and serve in practice to increase the number of farmers with outside jobs. If industrialization means higher land prices, it is not an economical proposition for other farmers to increase the size of their farms by buying up the land of those families who have left farming.

Furthermore, it is the local inhabitants, including the farmers, who are required to make the preliminary investments for regional industrial development. The farmers must resign themselves to paring down the money spent on their farms in order to squeeze out the funds needed to encourage the building of factories and other aspects of regional development. It is unduly optimistic to suppose that the money spent now will increase future revenue and come back to the farmers; it seems safer to suppose that in the industrialized cities and towns new financial demands will eat up any increase in revenue and that no adequate consideration will ever be given to the needs of agriculture.

Thus, it seems unlikely that regional development will offer a way out for agriculture. Although the development of industry ought to be a means of contributing to the welfare of the inhabitants of the region, in practice so much emphasis is put on the means that the end is completely forgotten. It is a serious question for all inhabitants of the region—except the few who share the benefits of industrialization—and it is of particular importance to the farmers.

What will happen, then, if neither agricultural policy nor regional development serve to brighten the outlook for agriculture and the rural communities? If present trends continue, will farmers be driven more and more to find supplementary employment and the farms left to go to seed? Obviously this cannot be allowed. Regional development is necessary, as was the structural improvement of agriculture. The reason why both of them seem unattainable goals is because structural improvement was begun with an insufficient view of what could be done for agriculture and the agricultural communities, and because regional development has confused ends with means and become preoccupied with the question of economic growth.

IV. The Future of Agriculture and Trends in the
Agricultural Communities

This gloomy view of the future of Japanese agriculture is not the
only possible one. There also exists a comparatively optimistic view;
and during the past two or three years the prevailing tendency has
been to see the long-term outlook as bright. In the optimistic view,
the past few years' revolutionary population drift away from the
land will continue in the future; although, at the moment, the number of farming households is not decreasing in proportion to the
drift, a decrease has begun and will become still more marked in the
future.

Such observers differ in their estimate of the extent of the decrease, but they are alike in drawing their conclusions from the
sharp drop in the number of young people going into agriculture.
The statistics indicate that very few young people are going straight
from school into agriculture. At present, only one farm in five has its
future owner engaged in agriculture, and even if we include those
cases where the successor is still at school, the figure is likely to remain
at about one in four. This means that when the present farmer gets
too old to work—and the next generation should take over—the
family will cease to be a farming family, there will be a big drop in
the number of farming households and a marked increase in the
size of farms. If one adopts this view, then even at the most conservative estimate the number of farms will have been reduced by
half within thirty years and may drop to less than one million.

That the number of farm families will decrease is almost certain.
In addition to tendencies which have already begun—the depar-
ture of whole families from forest villages and the conversion of
farmland into residential districts on the outskirts of towns—I believe there will be a more general decrease in the number of farm
households. I also believe that there will be no sharp decrease of
the kind optimistically foreseen unless the following conditions are
fulfilled.

First, jobs must be available outside agriculture which will guar-
antee a stable livelihood. Unless it is possible for a family to live on
wages alone, without supplying its own rice and vegetables, the
predicted shift from agriculture will not take place. Second, the
pension system must be extended or improved to provide minimum

guarantees for old people; without such guarantees, farmers will not give up the land which offers them some security. Third, something must be done about the present uncontrolled rise in land prices and drastic steps taken to deal with the land question in a way that will make it impossible to profit from sitting on land until the price rises. Along the same line, it is essential that the housing problem be solved so that those who leave the farm villages should not be driven back because they lack a decent place to live in the towns.

Other conditions could be cited but I feel these three conditions are minimum requirements. Can they be fulfilled in the near future? I feel that at the latest these questions should be solved by the time, thirty years from now, the next generation is ready to take over, but if the number of families is to have decreased sharply in thirty years time, these conditions will have to be fulfilled much more quickly. I do not see how this is possible.

To take this view, however, does not mean rejecting the optimists' idea of reducing the number of farms and increasing their scale nor does it indicate a desire to arrange things so that the petty farmer can earn a livelihood without taking on other work. A decrease in the agricultural population and the number of households is an inevitable historical trend, and to resist it represents a kind of neo-physiocracy. The formulistic view of agriculture still harbors a kind of latent, unintentional physiocratism. The left-wing parties also try to retain the poor farmers as the basis of agricultural policy: they attack methods for improvement of the agrarian structure as seeking to "wipe out the poor farmers" and talk of cooperative management as the solution. In fact, as things are in Japan, even the upper stratum of farmers must cooperate if they are to have any future. The approach of Japanese government leaders, too, is still based on a belief in the pre-eminence of agriculture which includes all farmers but which has long concerned only 30 per cent of them. Where agricultural products are concerned, agricultural policy must, of course, cover all farmers; but where human beings are concerned, labor policy should cover the part-time farmers who are employed in permanent-waged occupations, and the farmers who work as day laborers or seasonal migrants are properly the concern of the Welfare Ministry. Agriculture must be freed from the shackles of the formulistic view of the poor farmer and from neo-physiocracy. A solution can hardly be expected by focusing attention on agriculture and relying on the energy of the poor farmer to tide things over. The farm of 2.5 hectares (just over six acres) which was the basic premise of the Fundamental Law of Agriculture allowed a farmhousehold with three working members an income equivalent to a single worker in industry, while even the so-called "wealthy farmers" are more akin to poor farmers.

Despite this, the wealthier farmers persist in looking to the agricultural policies of the Conservative party to improve farm management. Many of them mistrust the policies of the present government, yet they continue to rely on personal politics based on local loyalties to further their interests, and they support the Conservative party. On the other hand, those farmers who have comparatively stable secondary occupations have no positive interest in agriculture, and their political activity confines itself to a leaning toward the parties of the left, via their trade unions, at election-time. Most farmers with secondary occupations of the first type, who fall between these two groups, have insufficient land to farm for profit and are unable to concentrate on their secondary occupations; they are usually too busy to have any leisure for politics. (In personality they tend to be the most traditional and conservative, precisely the stratum which shows the political apathy supposedly typical of farmers.) In practice, they are at the beck and call of the wealthy farmers and vote for the Conservatives without ever formulating any clear-cut political views of their own; even the farmers who, as wage-workers with land of their own, are comparatively secure have little ambition to bring them over to their own views. Thus it seems probable that the impetus for a political fulfillment of the conditions listed above will not come from the farmers as a whole.

If the trend toward secondary occupations continues, it is to this trend itself that one should look for the key. The relative economic stability of the farmers with permanent-wage jobs tends to make them into a brake on the labor movement. The white paper on agriculture shows that the number of permanently employed who commuted from the farms in January 1963 was 3,340,000, or 17 per cent of the total permanently-employed population in Japan. The future course taken by Japanese agriculture and the agricultural communities will be determined, I feel, by whether it proves possible to arouse these commuting workers and the younger generation of full-time farmers who still dream of progress. There are those of the younger generation who have still not despaired, who still hope to carry through an agricultural revolution and who cherish a deep dissatisfaction with the solid barrier that stands in its way.

PART II
SURVEY REPORTS

1. VILLAGE LIFE IN CENTRAL CHINA

As an assistant of Professor Megumi Hayashi, former chairman of the Sociology Department of the University of Tokyo, I made several agricultural surveys near Suchow in central China. In 1946, just after the war, I published a book entitled *Chūgoku Nōson Shakai no Kōzō* (The Social Structure of Chinese Agricultural Society),[1] which contains studies of central and northern Chinese rural society based on my own research and that of Japanese and foreign scholars. The Suchow area survey report itself was written by Professor Hayashi and incorporated in his book *Chūshi Kōnan Nōson Shakai Seido Kenkyū* (Research on Central Chinese Rural Social Systems).[2]

The following is a brief report of the survey we made in central China from 1940 to 1943. Since the rural situation has been completely changed under the post-war Communist government, this report can only sketch the traditional Chinese village.

I. OUTLINE OF THE SURVEYED VILLAGE

Fengchiao lies approximately four kilometers west of Suchow; both are located in the southern delta of the Yangtsu River. Fengchiao is renowned for its view of the Grand Canal, which joins the Yangtsu River east of the town, as well as for its 1,400 year old Han-shan temple.

Fengchiao Creek bisects the town, flowing in front of the Han-shan temple, and eventually joins the Grand Canal. We surveyed the villages laid out on the creek's west side. Administratively, these villages belonged to Fengchiao town in the second ward of Wu prefecture; the prefectural offices are located in Suchow. Fengchiao as an administrative district contains 1,869 households composing

---

[1] The first edition was published by Taigadō in 1946; the second and enlarged edition by Yūhikaku in 1953.

[2] Yuhikaku, 1953.

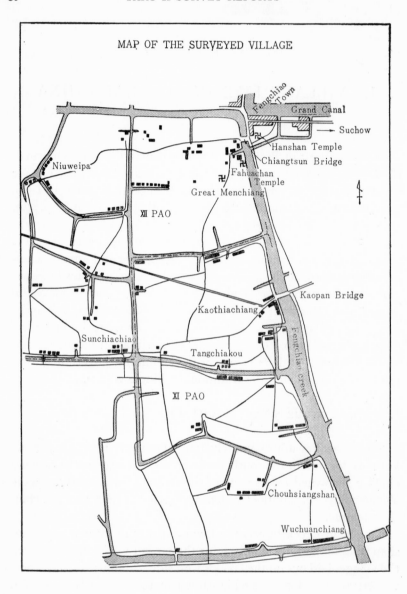

MAP OF THE SURVEYED VILLAGE

Fengchiao Town

Grand Canal

→ Suchow

Hanshan Temple

Chiangtsun Bridge

Niuweipa

Fahuachan Temple

Great Menchiang

XII PAO

Kaopan Bridge

Kaothiachiang

Sunchiachiao

Tangchiakou

Fengchiao Creek

XI PAO

Chouhsiangshan

Wuchuanchiang

160 *chia*[3] and 15 *pao*; our survey area included the eleventh and twelfth *pao*. The *pao-chia* administrative system often does not coin-

[3] Under the *pao-chia* system ten households constitute a *chia* under a *chia*-chief and ten *chia* constitute a *pao* under a *pao*-chief. The *pao* belongs to a *chen* (town) or *hsiang* (village), a *chen* being a town of over one hundred households.

cide with the actual units of the community, since creeks divide the villages naturally. Villages on opposite river banks but connected by bridge are often administered separately although they actually operate as one village. We chose the two surveyed *pao* for convenience' sake and, when necessary, we extended the survey to Shihshan, a neighboring village. The surveyed area belonged, in fact, more naturally to Shihshan than to Fengchiao and was incorporated as the seventh and eighth *pao* of Shihshan village in 1943.

Distant hills are visible to the west and south of the surveyed area, but here the villages are stretched over flat farm land. The farming area is crisscrossed by creeks; streams of all sizes connect numerous lakes and marshes, providing important routes for the transportation of goods. The smaller streams can also carry boats but contribute more by supplying water for irrigation and grassy silt for fertilizer. Without the rice from this area, it is said, all of China would starve, and without these creeks the rice produced here would be negligible.

Agricultural hamlets are strung along the banks of the rice field within these creeks. Large concentrations of hamlets form in the knots of the major channels, but rural hamlets are generally small, the largest in the surveyed area had only fourteen houses.

Most of the surveyed area was originally called Sunchia, but following the Taipintse Revolt, immigrants from other areas replaced the original inhabitants, whose surname was Sun. These immigrants from southern China have converted a former residential area adjacent to Fengchiao into fields producing sweet potatoes and horse beans. Rice paddies are everywhere except for the occasional clusters of graveyards for nearby Suchow's wealthy residents. Rice is the summer crop and wheat the winter crop, although vegetables are sometimes cultivated instead of wheat.

Farmhouses are one-storied, often with several families sharing one rectangular building. Most houses are roofed with tile, although non-farmers, new residents, and the poorer peasants roof their homes with thatch. The comparatively large Fahuachan Temple and Great Mengchiang Shrine are easily recognizable among the flat, one-story houses. The nunnery and smaller Menchiang shrines in the area are not large enough to stand out above the ordinary farmhouses.

The surveyed village contains 209 households and includes the eleventh *pao* with 10 *chia* and the twelfth *pao* with 8 *chia*. *Chia* correspond closely to the number of hamlets in the area. Among the 209 households, 154 houses, or 74 per cent of the total, are engaged in agriculture. The remaining houses, or the non-farmers, are scattered throughout the area with concentrations in the Chiangtsun and Kaopan Bridge areas. Twenty-five types of occupation are found among the non-farmers; the major ones include 8 factory workers, 7 rice-straw board makers, 4 agricultural day-workers, 3 osier-basket makers, 3 small businessmen, 2 tailors, and 2 butchers; the others include Buddhist priests, moralists, school teachers, and plasterers. The Huashing Paper Factory in the thirteenth *pao* employs the eight workers mentioned above while most of the Yenchow immigrants make the rice-straw board. Finally, four jobless families receive support from relatives and neighbors, and three householders work in other parts in the country.

II. ECONOMIC STRUCTURE OF THE FARM HOUSEHOLDS

The 154 farm households in the surveyed area cultivate a total of 1,556.3 *mu*, 1,309.8 *mu* of which are paddy fields and 246.5 *mu* upland field. The average cultivated area per house is 10.1 *mu*, a little smaller than the general average for the entire area, because proximity to the city permits a number of the farmers to have outside jobs. Additionally, a number of poorer farmers live in the surveyed area.

Social stratification based on the extent of cultivated land reveals that 41 per cent of the farm families have less than 5 *mu* while only 33 per cent hold more than 10 *mu*. No family cultivates over 40 *mu*.[4] Farmers with less than 10 *mu* have difficulty supporting themselves even though they may own their own land. Only 11 per cent of the cultivated land, or 177.5 *mu*, is owned by the cultivator. The breakdown, as shown in Table 1, reveals only nine owner-farmers; tenant-farmers represent two-thirds of the total population; the village can be considered almost a tenant village.

---

[4] The largest landowner, 38.1 *mu*, grows sweet potatoes in the upland fields. The largest paddy-field farmer's land is 35 *mu*. We ought to distinguish between paddy and upland field because of the difference in income, but we ignore the difference in our table because there are only a few upland fields owned by villagers in this area.

Creek near Fengchiao   (China)

Villagers Hulling Rice (China)

Hamlet and Paddy Field   (China)

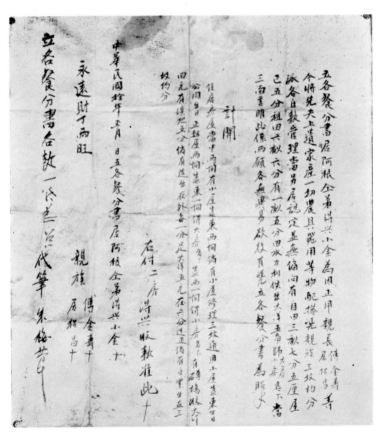

A Document Establishing a Family Division   (China)

TABLE 1.   Composition of Farming Households

Size of Cultivation (in mu) / Farmer-type	−2	−5	−10	−15	−20	−25	−30	30−	Total
Landowner lending over 3 mu	2	3							5
Owner-farmer	2	2							4
Owner-tenant	2	6	9	8	1	5	6	4	41
Tenant	7	40	27	14	7	8	1	1	105
Full-time farmer	1	18	23	17	8	13	7	4	91
Part-time farmer (A)	1	23	11	5				1	41
Part-time farmer (B)	10	10	2						22
Total	12	51	36	22	8	13	7	5	154

Part-time farmer (A): farming is the main occupation.
Part-time farmer (B): farming is the supplementary occupation.

Absentee landlords control most of the tenant-farming land. The two local landlords lend 21.2 mu and 32.1 mu. Land owned within the community comprises only 17 per cent of the total farm land; the largest percentage is controlled by urban absentee landlords: 59 per cent by Suchow residents, 10 per cent by Mutu town residents, and 8 per cent by Fengchiao residents. Suchow's percentage includes 10 per cent prefectural-government property, 8 per cent clan property, 4 per cent business firm and bank property, and 3 per cent charitable clan property.

Land is borrowed and rented under the tenancy system characteristic of this area. A tenant-farmer must pay 40–45 per cent of their rice crop as rent, but he has a recognized right of cultivation. The landlord retains the subsurface rights and the tenant has the surface rights of the land. As long as a tenant pays his rent, his right of cultivation may be inherited by his sons, sold, mortgaged, or temporarily sub-lent to raise money—all without interference from the owner. This surface-right clause is found in 256 tenant contracts of a possible 273 paddy fields in the surveyed village. Only twelve of the forty-three upland fields have no surface right, five of them are used as graveyards and are paid for by service rather than by rent.

Although the right of tenancy remains generally stable, high rents prevent the tenant-farmer or even the owner-tenant farmer from earning a sufficient living. Accordingly, 43 per cent or 63 farmers in the surveyed area have supplementary occupations. Farmers whose part-time labor provides the majority of their income number 22 persons, including 9 agricultural day-workers and 5 factory workers. Other farmers with part-time employment include 12 osier-basket makers, 4 tailors, 3 plasterers, 2 teahouse proprietors, 3 factory workers, and 7 agricultural day-workers.

The largest number, sixteen, of farmers with supplementary occupations are employed as agricultural day-workers. Eighty-three, or 54 per cent, farmers employ part-time help and may themselves be so employed. Nine well-to-do farmers employ full-time agricultural laborers, 2 more employ seasonal laborers, and 3 farmers co-employ one seasonal worker.

Thus, in this area, we may roughly divide the farmers into two categories: wealthy farmers with large tracts of land employing agricultural laborers and marginal farmers with small land holdings maintaining a subsistence living.

The possession and use of buffaloes in the surveyed area point up the immense disparity between the wealthy and marginal farmer groups. Since the water level of the creeks and the land within them remains generally at 1.5 meters, buffaloes are absolutely necessary for irrigation. Only 24 families have their own buffalo; some families own a few buffaloes in common, but both of these groups number only 45 families. Sixty-five per cent of the farmers engaged in rice paddy cultivation who rely on the use of buffaloes to irrigate their fields must pay for the use of this beast by their own labor.

TABLE 2.   Stratification of Farming Households

Stratification \ Farmer-type	Landlord	Wealthy farmer	Middle-class farmer	Petty farmer	Employed laborer
Owner-farmer	2	—	1	5	1
Owner-tenant	—	8	19	11	2
Tenant	—	1	29	69	6
Full-time farmer	1	8	42	40	—
Part-time farmer (A)	—	1	7	33	—
Part-time farmer (B)	1	—	—	12	9
Total	2	9	49	85	9

Table 2 outlines the farmer stratification which we have just explained. Sixty-one per cent of the surveyed group fall into a class of petty or hired farmers constantly suffering from poverty. Moreover, seventy-nine, a little more than 50 per cent, farmers hold debts. The wealthier farmers contract debts also, but these are often for purchases of paddy fields and buffaloes. Of the debts, however, 79 per cent are for unproductive uses such as funeral services (30 cases) and maintainence of minimal living conditions (27 cases).

About one-half of the farmers in the area live constantly in a critical situation. Living expenses climb with one's social position, but the wealthier farmers commonly organize *chienhui* or *chianghui* (mutual savings and aid associations), which provide funds for emergencies, or can rely on emergency financial aid from friends and relatives.[5] Middle or lower class farmers can not benefit from such mutual aid associations and consequently lead a precarious, marginal existence. Such daily uncertainty may explain the widespread belief in superstition among the poorer peasants.

III. FAMILY LIFE AND THE CLAN SYSTEM

The 209 families in the surveyed village include 449 males and 430 females, averaging 4.2 persons per family. The 154 farm families include 376 males and 366 females, averaging 4.8 persons. This average of less than 5 members per family is not peculiar to the surveyed village but corresponds with the general trend in central China. Among those families surveyed, the largest had 13 members, the majority 4 members. Families with 3–6 members constituted 70 per cent of the total. In a status count, family heads, their wives and children totaled 80 per cent of the population. Kinship structure is comparatively simple. Large families including married collateral relatives rarely exist in central China, a significant difference from the north Chinese peasant families with their complex kinship structure. In the surveyed area, one-couple families were 66 per cent, families with no couples 22 per cent, and thus families with three or more couples only 14 per cent of the total number.

The family unit recognizes no set pattern in the authority of the family head (*tangchia*). The family head guides the sale and division

---

[5] Because of economic changes, the number of such associations has decreased. At the time of our survey only two remained in this area, although many similar associations, operating under various means, had sprung up.

of the family property and makes marriage arrangements for family members, but he never acts independently or arbitrarily. He always discusses matters with his wife and adult children. Although the status of the female is generally lower than the male's, the housewife's status is rather high, and her opinion influences the family head. Among the poorer farmers in particular, female status is high since the female family members are important not only as agricultural laborers but also as part-time laborers making osier-baskets and embroidering articles.

Peculiarities of the Chinese family system are best shown in its inheritance structure. Equal property partition among the male members of the household is strictly observed among the farm families. Property division may take place either before or after the death of the father but generally occurs at the time of the marriages of the second and third sons, as harmonious family life is difficult to maintain when married brothers live together. All kinds of property, farm appliances, domestic animals, movable property, and liabilities as well as estates and buildings, are divided equally under the supervision of family relatives. Occasionally, the division is conducted by lottery. As far as possible, each successor receives an equal share; and sometimes differences in crop yields form an important aspect of property partition. When small homes are partitioned, the living room is usually a communal room and the other rooms are divided equally. Documents of property partition are often drawn up among middle and upper class peasants. Petty farmers, who often lack enough land to divide, allow one son to cultivate the land; he must then pay rent to his brothers engaged in other occupations for the use of the land. After property partition, each son establishes an independent household. If the parents are still living, the sons leave some fields for their exclusive use or pay them an equal amount of food and money. The eldest son, in theory, does not receive any larger share of the property than his younger brothers, although we found several cases where the eldest brother received a little more as his son's share.

In China, the principle of clan exogamy, *i.e.* non-marriage between identical surnames, is practiced except when the partners are of different genealogy. Girls always marry out and, theoretically, the husband of one of the daughters cannot succeed the family. Usually, a son of one of the brothers of the family head will succeed to a family which does not have a male heir. We learned in our survey, however, that a number of husbands who married into the family succeeded the family. Numerically, eight out of 104 couples were of this type. Occasionally, if the family is wealthy enough, some property is given to the nephew who has the right of succession.

The average marriage age is 21.5 years for males and 18.7 years for females. Engagements are arranged early, the youngest at age 6, the average between ages 10 and 15 for the middle and upper classes. We recorded eight cases of *tungyanghsi* where a girl lives with the family of her future husband. One couple was already married but the rest were not. *Tungyanghsi* are taken by middle class farmers to supply additional labor and to economize wedding expenses.

Although weddings are occasionally quite expensive, their cost can be prearranged. Funeral expenses, on the other hand, are not always expected. In our survey area, thirty families borrowed money for funeral expenses, because elaborate funerals are considered a sign of filial piety. Post-funeral religious ceremonies, however, are not considered important. Not all families maintain the wooden ancestor tablets, and fewer yet own the *chiatang* in which the tablets are traditionally preserved. Surprisingly, the eldest son does not always succeed to the maintenance of the *chiatang*. In the typical farm family where property is partitioned equally among all the sons, ancestral religious services are clan and not family ceremonies.

The *tsungtsu* (clans) in the surveyed area appear small and powerless, a possible consequence of the devastation of the village during the Taipingtse Revolution. The largest clan is the Kao clan incorporating seven families. There are two clans which include six families; one, five families; four, four families, etc. Clans with relatively influential and wealthy backgrounds are the six Wang families of Tangchiakou and the four Chu families of Niuweipa. But neither the Wang nor the Chu clans have clan property or clan ancestral shrines. They have neither *tsupu*, genealogical records, nor do they perform special clan religous services.

Yet even such clans retain some clan consciousness. All clan members readily identify the oldest member of the oldest generation as the clan chief. The chief performs no specific functions, and there is no real need for the small clan to maintain clan unity under the chief. Clan consciousness arises spontaneously if a small clan group lives in close proximity. Clan members of the same generation use identical name characters (for example, Chu Chuangsheng, Chu Lungsheng, Chu Shuansheng, and Chu Jensheng). Clan members co-own their buffaloes; they help each other during special occasions like weddings and funerals. All are expected to join in mutual relief projects. Clan members act as witnesses when one of its members sells, purchases, or mortgages land.

Normally, such mutual aid tends to remain within the immediate kinship group. Surprisingly, in case of debt, a peasant usually relies on his wife's relatives rather than his own kinsmen. The clan has no influence even in those cases where a daughter's husband succeeds the family. One case was recorded where a widow, being unfriendly with her own clan members, adopted a son from an unrelated family to succeed her family, and the clan was powerless to restrain her. Although such an instance indicates the family's limited land resources, it dramatizes further the weak cohesion and control of the clan. References are always made to clan control in a land deed but such expressions tend to be stereotyped and lacking in conviction. Hsiao-Tung Fei wrote concerning a central Chinese village, "The *tzu* (clan) can be taken as no more than a ceremonial group which assembles periodically at wedding and funeral occasions... real social obligations of mutual aid exist between smaller groups, such as brothers with newly divided households."[6] His comments hold true for our surveyed village as well.

IV. VILLAGE LIFE AND POWER STRUCTURE

Settlements in the surveyed village are small hamlets of less than fifteen households, grouped into *chia*. Each hamlet is a small community in which members have direct and daily contact with each other; members of the *chia* loan each other farming appliances and help in cultivating the land. These hamlets form the unit of social life for their inhabitants.

Hamlets are not, however, self-sufficient social groupings. The small teahouse in the village is an institution for the exchange of news and gossip; middle and lower farmers gather there particularly

[6] Hsiao-Tung Fei, *Peasant Life in China*, London: George Routledge and Sons, 1939, p. 85.

during slack seasons. There are three such teahouses in the southern, central, and northwestern sections of the surveyed village. We may consider these teahouses as centers of areas larger than each hamlet. Although the administrative *pao* have little influence over village life, such settlements form a second unit of social life, complementing the neighborhood hamlets. Village mutual aid and saving associations are organized in such an area, and members gather from throughout the area to celebrate weddings and funerals.

Religious congregations are also often formed on an inter-hamlet basis. The farmers revere Menchiang, a protector of crops, a killer of bandits, and a deity of bumper crops. Menchiang shrines and shrine associations (*hui*) are found throughout this region; the Menchiang shrine near the Chiangtsun Bridge is the center of the Great Menchiang Hui which has members all over the area. Smaller shrines and associations have been built in different parts of the village; interestingly, the *hui* are usually found in the area of the local teahouse.[7]

The poorer farmers, however, are not allowed to participate in these religious associations. Membership is limited; the members rotate duty at the shrine festivals, a function beyond the means of the poorer farmer. Non-members may go to see the festivals and be treated with appetizers and tea but may not participate in them. Festivals are not celebrated for the community as a whole but for associations with particular members. Small farmers and day-laborers are not necessarily excluded from the associations, but they lack the money necessary to participate in them.

Tutimiao (a local earthly deity) is the god of every resident in the territory of its jurisdiction. The *tutimiao* in this district, however, is enshrined in Hoshan, some distance from the surveyed village, and its jurisdiction covers a large area. The villagers pay homage to the shrine for charms which they worship in their homes and give money offerings to the lower *miao* (shrine) employee in March. Neither of these practices, however, requires the group participation of the villagers. For the social life of the village, the important factor is the Menchiang religious celebrations.

[7] Other religious associations include a Taoist group; Yangfuhonwang Hui organized by a group of immigrants from southern China for the deity of their original home; two women's Buddhist associations, one organized around a nunnery and the other organized by a priest of the Great Menchiang Shrine.

Thus, the power structure of the rural community, too, is firmly restricted by economic power. Although a big landlord's property may be divided, his resources will have been accumulated for generations, and a family may then maintain communal power. Where there is no such family in control, a wealthy farmer of ability may easily gain the leadership of a village, as has happened in Fengchiao.

When we surveyed the village, the leaders were two men who had been *pao*-chiefs: one was from the Chu family of Niuweipa and the other from the Wang family of Tangchiakou. They were both owner-tenant farmers—wealthy but not of the highest class. Leaders because of their talent and capability, both were able to read and write and had been collectors of farm rent (*tsuichia*) on behalf of a few Suchow landlords.[8] During the war the government abolished the *tipao* system of collecting land tax and asked Mr. Wang to collect the land tax and the rent of this area.[9]

Thus they became the *pao*-chiefs and assumed authority as political and administrative leaders. They control village affairs by consulting with the wealthier and more talented farmers; no consideration has been given to the opinion and attitudes of the majority of poorer farmers. Local autonomy under the *pao-chia* system is a formality. No municipal tax is collected, and there is no active village administration. The position of the *pao*-chief may thus be a nominal office; there has been no exploitation of the village farmers by the *pao*-chief to aggrandize his position.

At the same time, these officials have never exerted themselves on behalf of the small farmers and day-laborers. Since there is a high farm employment turnover in the village, no feelings of concern and interest between employer and employee have developed. This is also true for relations between the wealthy and poor farmers.

[8] The ability to read and write is a critical tool for leaders in the surveyed village. Among the residents 16 years of age or over, we found only 8.3 per cent male and 0.3 per cent female literacy. The percentage of elementary school attendance, however, was 39 per cent male and 7 per cent female (ages 5–15).

[9] The *tipao*, the land-tax collector, has greater power where the farmers are owners. Where the majority are tenant farmers as in the surveyed village, the *tsuichia*, assigned to collect the farm rent from landlords and corporations, has greater power. The *tipao* in our area was a middle-class farmer who was not prominent.

V. Town and Local Administration System

Economically, the life of the villagers is not self-sufficient, and they must purchase many goods in Fengchiao. The shops and professions in Fengchiao are as follows: 6 general stores, 7 butchers, 4 teahouses, 3 flour factories, 4 rice shops, 3 liquor shops, 2 bean-curd shops, 1 rice-cake shop, 1 Chinese cake shop, 1 cigarette shop, 2 smiths, 1 carpenter, 1 soy-sauce factory, 1 oil pressing factory, 3 cloth shops, 1 druggist, 1 incense-stick shop, 2 bamboo dealers, 5 barber shops, 3 tailors, 1 funeral-goods shop, 2 fish dealers, 4 shoe shops, 1 ceramic repair shop, 1 doctor, and 1 fortune teller.

These shops and professions can supply nearly all the daily necessities of the farmers. The wealthy farmers purchase little in Suchow and a negligible amount from the small general stores in the hamlets. Many of the farmers even purchase vegetables at the morning fair held along Fengchiao's narrow streets; 20 per cent of the rice farmers do not produce enough for their own consumption and must buy staples.[10] The markets for the rice farmers are the town's rice shops; sweet potatoes are sold in special shops opened at harvest time in the town. Colza, produced in small quantities, is converted into edible oil at the oil pressing factory; only horse beans are brought into Suchow's vegetable market. Agricultural products are sold primarily in Fengchiao, and strong economic ties have grown up between the village and the town.

Except during the busy season, the upper and upper-middle class farmers go marketing in town every morning. It is the man's job, not his wife's; on the way home from the market—vegetables, meat, and fish in hand—they drop in the teahouse to chat and exchange news. The wealthy go to town again in the afternoon to rest at the teahouse, sometimes to play mahjong. The teahouse in Fengchiao is a place where prominent villagers can meet townspeople and leaders from other villages.

As indicated previously, the town as a local autonomous body

[10] There are 130 rice-producing farmers of which 26 must bolster their harvest by purchasing rice. Ninety-four have surplus rice to sell; 10 families are barely self-sufficient. Until the war the majority of purchasers made 4 payments a year for the commodities; after the war, they paid in cash because the currency value had declined so rapidly.

consists of the surveyed village organized into two *pao*, Fengchiao organized as one *pao*, and neighboring villages grouped into 12 *pao*. *Pao*-chiefs are the town (*chen*) leaders. Each family is supposed to elect a *chiao*-chief, and the *chiao*-chiefs choose the *pao*-chief; but the position of *pao*-chief is always occupied by able and economically powerful men. Theoretically, the head of the administrative town is selected by the *pao*-chiefs, but in practice, the prefectural government appoints him. Such an arrangement undoubtedly satisfies the absentee landlords, who are an effective pressure group in prefectural politics. Since many of the *pao*-chiefs are the big landlords' rent collectors, the ruling class maintains a strong hold over local politics.

Although the town and villages constitute a local political unit, they actually play no active political role; rather, they form a terminal administrative organization of the government. The functions of the *pao-chia* are limited to compiling the *pao-chia* census, issuing prefectural residence cards, implementing the orders of the prefectural government, and collecting war funds. There are no other functions carried out by the town itself. Education is not the responsibility of the administrative town since the Fengchiao elementary school is a prefectural institution, and the other small schools are private. Residents are assessed for the municipal office rent and the town clerk's salary. War and municipal funds are assessed according to acreage of cultivated land, whether it is cultivated by the owner or a tenant. The landlord, of course, may pay the assessment from his high rents. Since these funds are levied on the village residents, absentee landlords may escape paying them altogether; owning lands in the village, they leave the burden of expense to the poorer farmers. Han-Seng Chen has pointed out that village and town politics are built on the power of the landlord,[11] which has proved valid in our survey.

---

[11] Han-Seng Chen, *The Present Agrarian Problem in China*, Shanghai: Institute of Pacific Relations, 1934, p. 19.

2. SOCIAL ORGANIZATION IN INDIAN VILLAGES

During the winter of 1962–63, Professors Tsutomu Ouchi, Chie Nakane, and the author visited India and surveyed two agricultural villages, one a West Bengal village in a wet paddy area and the other a village in a dry farming area in Gujarat State. As our visit was quite short, we were unable to make completely satisfactory surveys of the villages, but we felt that the data we collected were of sufficient interest to justify publication. After publication of the Japanese report, the author brought out an abridged English survey report entitled, "*The Socio-Economic Structure of the Indian Village;*" it was published by the Institute of Asian Economic Affairs in 1964.

The following survey reports are a part of the village organization survey conducted by the author.

A) A Village in a Dry Farming Area

I. A General Description of the Village

Going north from Bombay by express train for about six hours, we arrive at the city of Baroda in the center of the state of Gujarat. Baroda was the capital city of the kingdom of Baroda before Indian independence was declared. At present its population numbers almost 300,000, and it is the commercial and industrial center of the region. Samiala, the village which we had selected as our survey area, is located about 13 kilometers southwest of the city of Baroda· There is a well-surfaced road from Baroda to the entrance of the village, and a bus going to Padra, 3 km. beyond the village, passes about once an hour. There is also a narrow-gauge steam train service on a local line from Baroda. The track cuts across part of the village lands, but there is a fair distance between the center of the village and the nearest station on the line.

According to the census of 1951, Samiala village was a unit of local government comprising an area of 6.4 sq. km. The population was 1,400, made up of 334 households. Apart from a small settlement near the railway station, Samiala consists of three village agglomerations. The largest of these, containing about 230 households, is the main village of Samiala. The greater part of this agglomeration is located on the northern side of the road between Baroda and Padra, but a few families have moved as a result of road realignment works and now live across the road on the southern side. The little village of Laximipura, containing more than twenty households, is a small agglomeration located on the southern side of the road to Padra about 1 km. from the main village of Samiala. These two agglomerations have been included in the same unit of village government since early times, and Laximipura has been traditionally regarded as being under the control of the main village of Samiala. Lastly there is Gokulpura, an agglomeration of about sixty households, which we can reach from the main village of Samiala by going about 2 km. to the north, climbing a gentle slope into rolling country. This agglomeration is an offshoot of the large village of Bahili which is situated 4 km. north of the main village of Samiala. It was included in the local government unit of Samiala when the New Panchayat System was put into effect in 1952, but until that time it had been independent in matters of government as well as constituting a separate village.

The Social Education Organization Training Center attached to the University of Baroda is also located in the administrative area of Samiala village. Our survey was carried out with the co-operation of this Center, but its residents, together with those of the small agglomeration at the railway station, were excluded from our survey of the village. Our survey, therefore, covers three agglomerations— the main village of Samiala, Laximipura, and Gokulpura.

Before entering into a detailed analysis of the area surveyed, it will be well to present a general picture of the village. First let us establish the position of the surveyed area in the surrounding region, using for the purpose the statistics relating to the surveyed area in the 1951 census. These are given in Tables 1 and 2. In them the village of Laximipura is treated as part of Samiala village. The average figures for the administrative area of Baroda Thalka, to which the surveyed area belongs, are also given. These figures are averages of figures from 121 villages.[1]

TABLE 1.   Area, Number of Households, and Population

	Samiala	Gokulpura	Total	Average of Thalka
Area (sq. km.)	4.9	1.5	6.4	5.3
No. of Houses	264	49	313	232
No. of Households	274	60	334	246
Population	1,135	265	1,400	1,138
(Per household)	(4.14)	(4.42)	(4.18)	(4.61)
Males	596	134	730	602
Females	539	131	670	536
Illiterates	686	165	851	826
(%)	(60.5)	(62.2)	(60.8)	(72.8)
Males	281	59	340	382
(%)	(47.0)	(44.0)	(46.5)	(63.5)
Females	405	106	511	444
(%)	(75.0)	(81.0)	(76.4)	(82.5)

From the Tables it will be seen that the village under survey is above average in area and population, but it is a representative village for the region in question. The illiteracy rate is lower than average, and male illiterates in particular are few in number. This fact shows that the village, enjoying as it does the benefits of transport facilities, is in a fairly advanced state of urbanization. The low figure for the number of persons per household hints that greater population-changes have taken place in the village than in most villages. In other words, we may say that the surveyed village is one of the more advanced villages of the region.

If we now consider the population distribution according to occupations, we will see that the surveyed village has a non-agricultural population of 16.9 per cent, which means that the village has a high proportion of its population employed in agriculture, since the average percentage of non-agricultural occupations in the *thalka* stands at 31.3 per cent. In particular, the village of Gokulpura has

[1] It was not possible to use the results of the 1961 census, since these are still unpublished. The hierarchy of units of administration in Gujarat State is state-division-district-*thalka*. The surveyed area comes under Baroda Thalka in Baroda District, and is located at the western end of Baroda Thalka.

TABLE 2. Number of Persons Employed in Various Occupations

	Samila	Gokulpura	Total	Average of Thalka
Agriculture				
Land Wholly or	335	76	411	373
Mainly Owned	(29.5)	(28.6)	(29.4)	(32.8)
Mainly in Tenancy	315	44	359	166
	(27.7)	(16.6)	(25.6)	(14.6)
Agricultural	249	102	351	214
Labourers	(21.9)	(38.6)	(25.1)	(18.8)
Non-Cultivating	28	14	42	29
Landlords	(2.5)	(5.3)	(3.0)	(2.5)
Non-Agricultural				
Other Forms of	54	8	62	101
Production	(4.8)	(3.0)	(4.4)	(8.9)
Commerce	36	13	49	57
	(3.2)	(4.9)	(3.5)	(5.0)
Transport	13	0	13	62
	(1.1)	(0)	(0.9)	(5.5)
Other Services and	105	8	113	136
Miscellaneous	(9.3)	(3.0)	(8.1)	(11.9)

almost 90 per cent of its population employed in agriculture. When the autonomous village economy carried on in Indian agricultural villages under the *jajmani* system breaks up, the members of the village employed in handicrafts and service industries find themselves incapable of making a livelihood by their traditional occupations and they take up agriculture. For this reason, the fact that the village has a high agricultural population does not mean that it is a purely agricultural village in which the process of urbanization has been retarded. It is true that the agricultural population of the village is high in comparison with the villages in the immediate vicinity of the city of Baroda, but at the same time we must attribute the cause of this fact to the penetration of the commercial economy into the village and the consequent break-up of the village handicrafts.

Turning to agriculture itself, we will see that in the surveyed village the proportion of cultivating proprietors is fairly low, and that consequently the proportion of tenants and laborers is high. These figures reflect the state of the village before the implementation of the Land Reform, and the present state of the village is quite different. The categories into which the agricultural population is divided are also unsatisfactory in some respects. Nevertheless, these figures indicate that some degree of differentiation has taken place within the peasant stratum of the village. In particular, the number of non-cultivating landlords is not greatly different from that of other villages, but the number of tenants is so large that we must suppose that a fair amount of their land must have been owned by landlords living outside the village. This state of land-tenure has come about in response to the fact that the village is located comparatively near the city and to the fact that a commercial economy has developed in the area.

So far we have considered the outline description of the village which can be elicited from the census, but we must also remember that the caste system has an important significance in the Hindu village. Later we will analyse caste from various angles, but at this point it may be opportune to state the present position in the surveyed village on the basis of the data which we collected. These figures are given in Table 3. In the Table the castes are ranked in

TABLE 3.   Number of Households in the Various Castes

Caste	(Traditional Occupation)	Samiala	Laximipura	Gokulpura	Total
Brahmin	(Priest)	2	0	1	3
Bania	(Merchant)	1	0	0	1
Patidar — Dominant		32	0	13	45
Gosain	(Priest)	1	0	1	2
Kacchia	(Merchant)	3	0	0	3
Kumbhar	(Potter)	3	0	2	5
Luhor	(Blacksmith)	1	0	0	1
Baria		101	27	23	151
Valand	(Barber)	0	0	1	1
Bhoi	(Water-carrier)	1	0	1	2
Ravalia	(Rope-maker)	2	0	1	4
Rathod		4	0	1	5
Bhil		2	0	3	5
Vaghri	(Gardener)	4	1	12	17
Vankar	(Weaver)	26	0	15	41
Chamar	(Cobbler)	2	0	0	2
Bhangi	(Sweeper)	3	0	2	5
Muslims		39	0	0	39
Total		228	28	76	332

order, but this ranking is not conclusive. In particular, it is difficult to assign a definite ranking to the Kacchias and Luhors who have moved into the village from elsewhere. The traditional occupations of the castes have been added in the Table, but in many cases these occupations have been abandoned by the members of the castes. For example, the occupations of blacksmith and weaver are not carried on at all, and the majority of men in such castes are employed as agricultural laborers. Nevertheless, in spite of these changes, the castes and their hierarchical order of precedence are still to be found in the surveyed village, and the ranking of the castes shown in Table 3 is still, on the whole, recognized by the villagers in general.

It will be clear from the Table that the Patidars and Barias occupy a large proportion of the population of the surveyed village. If the Muslims, Vaghris, and Vankars are added to them, the total makes up about 90 per cent of the population of the village. Among these, the Patidars are cultivating proprietors or members of the upper stratum of those who oversee the management of agricultural holdings. The Barias, who number almost half the population, form a stratum extending over the middle and lower peasantry down to the agricultural laborers. The Vaghris and Vankars are agricultural and non-agricultural laborers. The upper stratum of the Muslims formerly constituted a class of tenant cultivators, but as a result of the Land Reform they have become cultivating proprietors and have risen to the middle stratum of the peasantry. These stratifications, of course, are only rough divisions of the population, but it may be useful to retain this image as an aid to understanding the analyses presented later. While the Barias occupy the overwhelming majority of households, the Patidars are the dominant caste and constitute the politically dominant stratum of the village.

In general these castes live in residential areas of their own, although some mingling of castes is also to be observed. In the main village of Samiala, as will be seen from the map, the Patidars live in the center of the village, in an area to the west and south of the square in front of the temple and *panchayat* office. The Muslims are collected together in an area to the west of the main area occupied by the Patidars. The most numerous caste, the Barias, have their houses enclosing these residential areas on the west and south. The Ravalias and Vaghris, who belong to the lower strata, have

Village Street in India (Gujarat)

Harvesting Tobacco Leaves (Gujarat)

Washing in the Pond   (Gujarat)

Potter   (Gujarat)

their houses in a small area to the southeast of the temple. The untouchable caste in the lowest stratum of the population lives in a
small separate agglomeration, divided from the rest of the village
by a small gully. Laximipura may almost be described as a one-
caste village of Barias, for the village includes only one Vaghri
household, and this is located a little distance from the others. The
village of Gokulpura was originally inhabited by Bhils, a tribal
people who took up residence as tenants of houses owned by Patidars. With the exception of one Bhoi household living in the Baria
section of the village, the caste distinctions in the pattern of housing
are much more clearly marked in Gokulpura than in Samiala. The
caste hierarchy is not only revealed by such residential segregation,
but also by the size of the houses and the quality of the materials
from which they are constructed. In both Samiala and Gokulpura
the houses in the Patidar sections are large houses, usually with tiled
roofs, which contrast sharply with the shabby, roughly-constructed
houses around them. Some houses in the Patidar section of Samiala,
however, are in a state of great dilapidation. These are houses inhabited by members of other castes, and if we compare this section
of Samiala with the Patidar section of Gokulpura, in which all the
houses are of the first class, we will be able to perceive the difference
in socio-economic organization between the two villages.

Finally, let us say a word about the geographical environment of
the village and its determining effect on the type of agriculture
which is carried on. The land of the village may be described as
level country with slight undulations, and in its natural condition
it is not the kind of plain-land which can be used for irrigated rice
culture. Only dry farming is carried on in the village. The main
crops are cotton, dry rice, *dhal* and other pulses, *bajra, jowar,* etc.
Besides these, vegetables, tobacco, and fruit (lemons, bananas,
mangoes, and *janful*) are produced in places where there are wells
for irrigation. Since the soil becomes very dry during the winter
season, well-irrigation is very important in the surveyed village.
The temperature remains high throughout the winter season, and
in this respect the conditions for agricultural production are amply
fulfilled. If only water were available it would be possible to use the
land at a high degree of intensiveness.

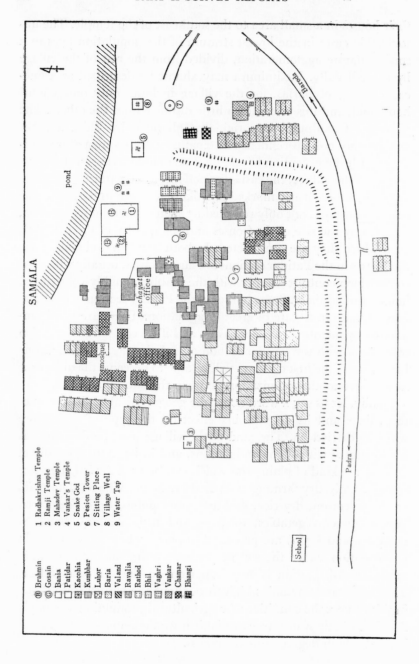

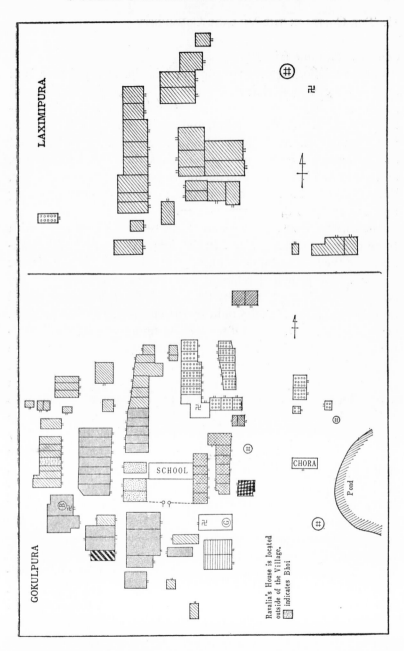

II. The Castes in the Village Community

Castes and the Caste Hierarchy

On the whole, the order of the castes in the surveyed area is as indicated by the dotted lines in Table 3; the Brahmins, Banias, and Patidars forming the upper stratum, the artisan castes and the Barias forming the middle stratum, and the Ravalias, Rathods, Bhils, and Vaghris forming the lower stratum. Beneath them is the lowest stratum made up of the untouchable castes, the Vankars, Chamars, and Bhangis. The Muslims do not form a part of the caste hierarchy, but it would probably not be a mistake to regard them as belonging approximately to the middle stratum.

Let us now give some account of these castes, beginning with those represented in Samiala. In Samiala, as elsewhere, the Brahmins are the sacerdotal caste and are, traditionally, in the highest stratum. The principal religious foundations in Samiala are the Radhakrishna Temple built by the King of Baroda, and the Ramji and the Mahadev Temples built by the villagers. To these we must add the Muslim mosque. Of the two Brahmins who live in the village, one lives in the Radhakrishna Temple and the other in the Ramji Temple. The former comes from a family which originated in the Surat area. His grandfather was a doctor, and his father took up residence in the temple about sixty years ago. Brahmins who succeed their fathers are known as Sadu-Brahmins, and they live a life regulated by religious law. They do not comb their hair, they do not shave their beards, and they do not eat food made from grain. Superficially, this man would appear to be a religious recluse, for he does not officiate at ceremonies of marriage or burial. However, since he cannot maintain himself on the Rs 131 per year granted him by the royal house of Baroda, he gets on his bicycle early every morning and rides to a textile factory in Baroda, where he earns Rs 100 per month for his officiation at a temple inside the factory. His father was a man of some consequence in village politics, and he himself has intervened in such matters to some degree, but his endeavors in this direction have now ceased. Respect is paid to him by the ignorant villagers of the lower strata, but a certain section of the higher-caste villagers are critical of him. The Brahmin who inhabits the Ramji Temple, on the other hand, is a poor wandering Brahmin who came from a village 155 miles to the north and took up residence in the then untenanted temple twenty-four years ago. Since the temple had been empty for a long time, the villagers had become parishioners of the Brahmins in the neighbouring villages of Kalali and Bil. One continuing consequence of this can be seen in the fact that the Brahmin must hand over half of the villagers' Kite Festival offerings to the Brahmins of Kalali and Bil. The Brahmin also visits three other villages in the vicinity, but only in the capacity of a substitute officiator at religious ceremonies. The fees which he receives for officiating at marriage and burial ceremonies are retained by him in their entirety, but this is not so in the case of rents paid by the cultivators of temple-owned land. The poor Brahmin's position in the village is typical of the position of similar members of the caste elsewhere—by virtue of being a Brahmin he is acknowledged to have a high status, but in daily life he can only maintain the style of living of the middle stratum of the village community.

The Banias, who rank second after the Brahmins, are represented in the village by only one family, and this family came into the village from elsewhere. The present head of the family, who was something of a landlord in the past, has a fair knowledge of English, and he fulfils the function of a mediator between the villagers and government officials.

We need not reiterate the fact that the most important of the castes in the upper stratum of the village community is the Patidar caste. We should suppose that the Patidars would not be a powerful group in Samiala, since the village comprises more than 230 families and the Patidars number only 32 families; but the economic stratification of the village is such that a comparatively large number of Patidars run large holdings, and it has made the Patidars the dominant caste in the village. They do not, however, monopolize political power in the village. In this region there are not a few villages in which the Baria caste is not only the numerical majority but also includes some households which are comparatively wealthy, and thus prevents the Patidar caste (which includes some poor men) from acquiring dictatorial power. The Patidars of such villages are known by the somewhat derogatory name of "Baria Patidars."

The Gosain and Kacchia castes, which come next to the Patidars in caste ranking, are all represented by families which have moved into the village during the present generation. The Gosain family moved in from a neighboring village in order to continue a deceased uncle's business. The three families of Kacchias moved in from Padra to establish small general stores in the village, and they live in rented houses.

Of the artisan castes, only two families of Kumbhars, or potters, are left in the village, and they do not have much significance in relation to the composition of the village. There is only one family of Valands, or barbers, and there is no need to give them special consideration. Consequently, the Barias account for almost half the number of families in the middle stratum of village population. The Barias in this village are divided into four descent groups, and they include certain persons who avoid the name Baria and call themselves Rajputs. Since these people belong to the Kshatria order in the *varna* division of society, they think themselves superior to the Patidars, but their economic power is not sufficient to command public acceptance of the idea. In terms of land-ownership, most of the Barias are in the middle and lower strata. Since the number of families included in this group is as much as three times the number of Patidar families—and among them there are some families which run holdings of considerable size—the caste is an important constituent of the village community.

Among the castes which make up the lower stratum the Ravalias were originally rope-makers, and even now they occasionally carry on this occupation, but since it is not sufficient to provide them with a livelihood they work as day-laborers or as drummers at marriage ceremonies and the Holi festival. The Rathods are agricultural laborers and also act as assistants to the village official in charge of police and tax-collection duties. The Bhils are a tribal people who have settled in the village, and four generations have passed since they first came into the village from a place thirty miles to the north. Because there are only a few families of them, they have become completely Hinduized. One of them is employed as a postman, and another is in charge of the electric pump at the village well. The Vaghris, whose traditional occupations are those of fruit-picking and gardening, are normally employed as day-laborers, but it is also customary for their womenfolk to do the washing-up at weddings and other celebrations and to receive the leavings of the feast. Thus we see that the four castes live in a state of dependence on the castes in the upper and middle strata of the village community.

The lowest stratum, the members of which live separated from the main village by a small gully, includes the Bhangis, who earn their livelihood as the village sweepers. They call at the village houses every evening after eight o'clock and receive the food scraps. Their social condition is similar to the unfree or depressed classes of feudal society. In contrast, the Vankars and Chamars are not so dependent on the village. This is especially true of the Vankars, whose traditional occupation was weaving, but who have now abandoned that occupation altogether and are employed as factory workers or go out to temporary work outside the village. Some of the women left behind keep water buffaloes for milking. Their economic condition is generally better than that of the poorer members of the middle and lower castes of the village community, and the area in which they live is relatively well-kept. The Chamars do, indeed, sometimes engage in the flaying of hides, but like the Vankars they look for work outside the village. The Vankars and the Chamars are known by the collective appellation "Dhed," and they consider themselves superior to the Bhangis. They consider the Bhangis to be the most untouchable of all the untouchables.

As has already been said, the Muslims may be regarded as belonging to the middle stratum of the village community. There has been a marked increase in the number of Muslim families, and since the land reform certain families among them have added to their economic power and are now playing a part in the dominant stratum of the village which cannot be ignored.

There is no need to give a special account of Laximipura, a one-caste village, but we shall give a general account of Gokulpura because it has structural characteristics which distinguish it from Samiala.

The Brahmin in Gokulpura maintains his family in the Ramji Temple, but because the village has few inhabitants and because the temple owns only a small area of land he spends most of his time in a near-by village of 300 families. The man is not in good health, and he has had to call upon the help of the Brahmin of Samiala. He has little influence in the village.

As in Samiala, the Patidars are the dominant caste in Gokulpura. There are twelve families of Patidars, and the greater part of them are wealthy; moreover, they have great family solidarity and constitute the overwhelmingly predominant power in village life. Al-

though their number is small in comparison with the Samiala
Patidars, there is no family or caste in the village which can stand
up against them; the Barias who are challenging the power of the
Patidars in Samiala are not so numerous in Gokulpura as to be able
to do the same there. The Barias number twenty-two families, less
than twice the number of Patidar families, and there are no particularly influential families among them. The Barias' subordination
to the Patidars is shown by the fact that, whereas the Patidars and
Barias of Samiala each have their own communal kitchens[2] for
marriage and burial ceremonies, in Gokulpura the two castes own
these facilities together.

The members of the Bhoi caste, who were originally water-car-
riers or chair-bearers, are now agricultural laborers. There is no
great difference between the members of the other lower-strata
castes and their counterparts in Samiala. It is worth pointing out
that a fair number of Vaghri families live in Gokulpura and that
they have their own temple in their section of the village. Because
there is a relative surplus of Vaghri families, a number of them go
outside the village to work.

Among the untouchables the Vankars of Gokulpura, like those of
Samiala, are no longer weavers but continue to work in the village.
The Samiala Vankars have a small temple-like erection of their
own, but in Gokulpura the caste is not so numerous, and they have
no such meeting place. They also consider themselves superior to
the two Bhangi families who live in their village.

Castes and the Village Community

It is said that the classical ideal of the Indian caste consists of
member solidarity and the formation of an inter-village caste *panchayat*. It is for this reason that the caste is frequently considered
a horizontal association which transcends the village and constitutes
a divisive force in Indian village society, and it is also for this reason

---

[2] Because large quantities of food are prepared for marriage and funeral
ceremonies, special cooking facilities are required. These facilities may be rented
to inhabitants of other villages or to members of other castes. However, members
of the non-vegetarian Rathod and Vaghri castes cannot use the kitchens. The
Muslims also own communal cooking facilities, but because the food they eat
differs from that of the other village inhabitants, they do not exchange cooking
facilities with the Hindu castes.

that efforts have been made to assess the relative strength of caste loyalty and village loyalty.

Our survey, however, was unable to find evidence of close caste solidarity transcending the village. For example, the caste *panchayat* to which the Samiala Patidars belonged was dissolved about twenty-five years ago and has never been reorganized.[3] The direct cause of the dissolution is said to have been a dispute occasioned by one of the members pocketing a sum of money levied as fines by the *panchayat*, but an underlying cause was the already weak horizontal solidarity of the caste.

Caste solidarity has been strong among the Banias because they comprise a small number of families and are economically secure. However, even the Bania caste *panchayat* has not been performing its functions for the past twenty years.

None of the members of the other castes had any recollection of caste *panchayats*. The Kumbhars have organized the Gujarat Potters' Association. Electing a chairman and eight committee members, they hold an annual general meeting in Baroda at which they debate their budget and accounts and have a good time. This body has lost the character of a caste *panchayat*, however, and may best be described as a trade association.

The absence of any strong caste solidarity transcending the village is also characteristic of Gokulpura. The Gokulpura Patidars have belonged to no caste *panchayat* for the last sixty years. It appears that the caste *panchayat* system disappeared at least half a century ago in this area and that the only activity of this kind has been the rare, informal meetings of the elders of the sub-castes which take place when it has been necessary to settle some matter.

These facts do not mean that caste solidarity within the village has been weakened. The caste structure of village society is still of some importance. The villagers are always conscious that there are certain people who are of their own caste as opposed to other castes, as well as being conscious that certain people are members of their own family or of their own *kutumb*. Although sectarian antagonism may arise within a caste, the members of the caste will continue to help each other and will maintain the collective ownership of the

---

[3] The Samiala member of the *panchayat* was a member of a family which has since become extinct. He was the most influential man in the village and held the office of headman for twenty years.

cooking facilities which symbolizes the communal nature of the caste. This is most clearly apparent in upper and middle strata castes.

For the same reasons, the members of these castes wish to preserve the distinctions between themselves and the castes of the lower and lowest strata. Class distinction between the Patidars in the upper stratum and the Barias in the middle stratum of society is not very obvious in the course of everyday life. The influential persons who appear at the various assemblies of the village will converse indiscriminately with Patidars and Barias. But members of the lower stratum castes do not aspire to take part in these assemblies, and if they did, the difference in the manner in which they would be treated would at once be apparent.

Class discrimination against the castes in the lowest stratum is so marked that it can be observed by anyone—as, for example, in the practices connected with drawing water from the village wells. Before the electric water-pump was installed, all the castes living on the west side of the small gully used the well next to the shrine of the Snake God, midway along the road from the eastern entrance of the village to the square in front of the temple. The Vankars and Chamars were not allowed to use this well, although it was near their houses, and they had to fetch water from a well located beside the railway, a somewhat greater distance away. This was a great hardship during the monsoon, when the gully became a watercourse, but they were pleased to have their own well. Although the Bhangis lived nearest the public well, they were not allowed to draw water from it, nor were they allowed to use the well belonging to the Vankars and Chamars. They had to get women from the other side of the gully to fill a small tank beside the public well for them, and they drew their water from this tank. Even when unobserved, no Bhangi ever drew water directly from the public well. Had any Bhangi been discovered doing so, it is certain that he would have been beaten and expelled from the village.[4]

Such class distinctions are also observed in Gokulpura. The Vankars have a well of their own, and the Bhangis must get the Vankars

[4] Even after the electric pump had been fitted to the public well and a piped water system installed, the Dheds and Bhangis had their water-taps placed some distance apart. The tap immediately beside the well could not be used by members of the village indiscriminately.

to draw water for them from that well. It is hard for the women to pull up the heavy water-jars, and recently many of them have been taking water from a well from which an electric pump supplies channelled water to irrigate the fields. The untouchables, however, cannot draw water directly from this well, and they are only allowed to make use of the channelled water.

The class distinctions are also observed by the village children. None of the children of the majority castes would ever go to play across the gully in the untouchables' section of the village. The son of a Patidar will mix on terms of equality with a Vankar boy in his high school class, but when they return to the village, they cannot address one another as members of the same species. Caste distinction of this kind is also observed between the Dheds and Bhangis, and although members of the two groups may live in neighbouring houses, their children never play together. Thus the Vankars and Chamars, discriminated against by those above them, discriminate against the Bhangis who occupy a still lower station than themselves.

The fact that members of the lowest castes are not considered members of the village community may be seen in connection with religious festivals. For example, the Vankars of Samiala have a small temple-like erection in their section of the village which is reserved for their own use. When the Bhangis need such an edifice, they make a miniature shrine out of mud-plaster. These people are also barred from participation in the many festivals celebrated by the village as a whole. For example, in celebrating the Diwali festival at the time of the Indian New Year, the untouchables perform their religious rites at their little shrine and not at the village temple. On the morning of the first day of the new year the Brahmins prepare food which they dispense to the villagers and receive offerings of money but the untouchables must wait outside the temple for the food to be brought to them.

Caste distinctions such as those relating to the untouchables fulfil the function of keeping up a consciousness of caste affiliation among the members of all the castes. It appears, therefore, that social divisions may arise on the basis of caste. Further, since the castes live in separate sections of the village, we may assume that there will be a tendency for consciousness of caste membership to take priority over consciousness of village membership.

But the village community is not fragmented by caste. There is no evidence in the surveyed area of that earlier state of rural society which was characterized by a high degree of economic self-sufficiency and in which the artisan and service castes were bound by the *jajmani* system in a state of dependence on the castes employed in agriculture. There is no evidence that tenants and agricultural laborers are permanently bound to their landlords by the conditions of their tenancy or of their employment. In spite of this, the solidarity of the village community is centered on the Patidars, the economically dominant caste and is the product of the cohesive force of the Patidars.

It is impossible for any villager to remain shut up in his own caste when all members of the village live in the same agglomeration, build their houses on land which may be regarded as belonging to the village, use a common well, enjoy the use of village-owned pastures (even if they are only of little value), use the village burning *ghat*, go out to work on village projects, and from time to time act as night-watchmen for the village. When the communal life of the villagers transcends caste, this transcending of caste must be accomplished under the direction and control of those persons and castes which hold superior economic power.

The dominance of the Samiala Patidars is not so strong, however, that they can afford to ignore the numerical majority of the Barias in the village and the increasing economic power of the Muslims. The fact that the Patidars enjoy a superior position in the caste hierarchy does not mean that they are using their traditional authority to oppress the Barias. When the castes in the middle stratum of society acquire some degree of power and when the solidarity of the castes in the upper stratum is divided by factions, opportunities arise for persons of the upper and lower castes to form associations which transcend the boundaries of caste, and these forms of association must lead to a lessening of class distinctions between the strata. The dynamics of the social organization of Samiala would appear to have developed along just such lines.

In contrast, when the castes of the middle stratum of society do not possess much power, the solid dominant caste will be able to contain them with ease, and its power as the dominant caste will be amply sufficient to control the entire village community. This is the situation in Gokulpura.

The majority of the members of the lower castes live in a state of dependence on the upper and middle castes. They do not comprise a large number of families, and since they are poor, they have no power. Even when they are fairly numerous, they own no land, and if they are not employed as agricultural laborers, they must go outside the village in search of work. Those who go outside the village to work are no longer a part of the village community, and they have no interest in the village. The same may be said of the untouchables in the lowest stratum of the society. The Vankars of Samiala comprise a fair number of families, but the majority of them earn their living outside the village. In their own village they live in a world of their own; they show no inclination to protest against the discriminatory treatment which they receive from the higher castes but direct their animosity at the Bhangis below them. The Bhangis, who are denied any opportunity of compensating for the oppression to which they are subject, are formally barred from membership in the village community, but have the "right" as village sweepers to beg food scraps of the upper and middle strata. They are like appendages to the village community. There is not yet the slightest trace of any resistance by the lower and lowest strata against the higher strata in the village.

III. VILLAGE SELF-GOVERNMENT

The Traditional Forms of Self-Government

The village owns a certain amount of property which is registered as "government land" or "public property," as shown in Table 4. The village as a whole is charged with the duty of maintaining and managing this property. It is also the duty of the village to look after the temples built by the villagers (as opposed to those which are owned by individuals or by castes) and to attend to their maintenance and the management of their lands. The village must also organize the many festivals which are associated with the temples.

It is also necessary for the village to levy corvée labor from the villagers when the village tank is to be repaired and to organize a night watch to stand guard over the crops in certain circumstances, such as crop failure. The village must also mediate in disputes between individual villagers so that order may be maintained. It is also possible for the village to pass judgment on villagers who disturb the peace and to require them to pay fines. Lastly, public works undertaken by the village are not always carried out by corvée labor, and it may collect subscriptions from the villagers to buy building materials.

TABLE 4. Government Land and Public Property

	Samiala (*incl. Laximipura*)	Gokulpura
Public Wells	3	2
Water Tanks	10	1
Grazing Land for Animals	4 (11.5 hectares)	1 (0.8 hectares)
Area of Village Housing Sites	(6.1 hectares)	(2.0 hectares)
Smashan (Burning Ghat)	1 (0.8 hectares)	1 (0.2 hectares)
Muslim Cemetery	1 (0.4 hectares)	—
Chora (Village Office)	1	1
Schools	1	1

In the past, village government was in the hands of the Patidars, and the Patidars still dominate the body of persons who administer the affairs of the temple. Formerly it was the practice for one of the influential Patidars to hold the office of headman and for him to be assisted by other influential Patidars. When any action was to be embarked upon in the name of the village, it was his duty to call an assembly of the *gram agewan* to advise him. This body consisted of leaders from the most powerful castes and residential areas. When necessary he also called an assembly of the *gram saba*, or general assembly of the villagers. The headman was given public recognition and authority by the external political authorities by means of an institution called the Police Patel.

The office of Police Patel still exists today, although the extent of its power is being progressively reduced. Summarizing the information which we obtained in interviews with the villagers, we may reconstruct the manner in which the system operated more than half a century ago. The Police Patel was the village headman, and he was endowed with wide powers. His official functions were (1) the maintenance of law and order in the village and (2) assistance to the tax-collector in the collection of the land tax. In the first case he was required to send periodic reports to the police regarding village births, deaths, and changes of residence. He also had to in-form the police of all reported offenses against the law. In the second, he was required to co-operate with the *talati*, the lowest official in the tax-collection system, and to take responsibility for the collection of taxes in the village. Around 1910, the Police Patel was paid Rs 70 per year by the Government for the performance of these duties, and he received a percentage-fee for collecting the land tax. In addition, before the transition to the New Panchayat System, the headman received an annual income of Rs 150 and was granted an area of land of more than one hectare.

The Police Patel was selected from *matadar* families who had the hereditary right of being eligible for the office of headman. The headman took office for a period of five years. The *matadars* assisted the Police Patel and administered the village. When we asked which families were *matadars*, we were told both in Samiala and in Gokulpura that they were all Patidars. At present there are four *matadar* families in Samiala, but about forty years ago there were five, one of the families having since died out. In Gokulpura there were two *matadar* families, but one of them has now died out. It was the general rule for the eldest son of these families to succeed to the status of *matadar*.

The *talati* is the tax-collecting official at the village level. In most cases he is a Brahmin. He brings the tax register up to date every five years and collects the taxes according to the established rate. The duties of the *talati* are not time-consuming, and his remuneration is low.[5] Because his remuneration is so low, the *talati* sometimes takes gratuities for his good offices in the sale of land, and he may take advantage of the ignorance of the peasants and engage in ingenious forms of professional misconduct. The system of tax collection by *talati* is still in force, but they are moved to other villages every two to four years in order to prevent malpractices.

The work of the *talati* is carried out with the assistance of the *valtania*, who act as messengers and odd-job-men for the Police Patel. The post of *valtania* is hereditary in three Rathod families in Samiala, and in Gokulpura it is hereditary in three Baria families. When the Police Patel wishes to call a meeting of the influential

[5] The basic salary of a *talati* ranges between Rs 46 and Rs 86. To this a cost-of-living allowance is added. The holder of the office of *talati* in the surveyed area is a man of 50 years of age who has served in this minor official post since 1925. His total monthly salary is only Rs 119, consisting of Rs 64 as basic salary and Rs 55 as cost-of-living allowance.

people in the village, it is a *valtania* who goes round announcing it, and he is present at the meeting, awaiting orders. If a government official should come to the village, the *valtania* may be called upon to assist him. In the same way, when the *talati* visits the village, a *valtania* must always be at his side and run errands at his command. The stick which a *valtania* always carries under his arm is the badge of his office. When there were three *valtania* in Samiala and two in Gokulpura, they took turns as nightwatchmen, but this arrangement is no longer in force.[6]

The traditional system of village self-government which we have described underwent some changes as a result of the resuscitation of the old *panchayat* system by the British colonial administration in 1920. The Kingdom of Baroda instituted *panchayat*s in each village. These *panchayat*s were not elected, but were nominated by the *matadar*s headed by the Police Patel at a meeting of the *gram agewan*. Although the *panchayat* was in general only a formal institution, in Samiala (as far as can be remembered) Barias were included among its members, and when the old *panchayat* system was in force, two of the five members came from that caste. In Gokulpura one of the five members was a Vankar. The lower caste member was only a nominal member in Gokulpura, but we may be right in thinking that in Samiala the participation of the lower caste members was a reaction to the break-up of the Patidars' dictatorship. We may take it that in Samiala, as elsewhere, the hereditary power of the *matadar*s vested in a small number of Patidar families had, in fact, crumbled and that members of the Baria caste were included in the *panchayat* because the number of families in their caste had increased so that they constituted a power which could not be ignored.

However, we cannot say that the revival of the old *panchayat* system brought about any marked changes in the traditional form of village self-government. This was because the old *panchayat* sys-

---

[6] In Samiala the salary of the *valtania* was Rs 9 to Rs 11 per month, and they were each granted about 0.4 hectares of land. In Gokulpura they received Rs 9 per month and were granted about 1.5 hectares of land. In 1961 there were two *valtania* in Samiala, but in 1962 the number was reduced to one, and he served as *valtania* in both Samiala and Gokulpura. His post ceased to be hereditary, and he received a salary of Rs 27 per month. The land which had been granted to the *valantia* as a hereditary reward for their services was in every case sold to them at nominal prices payable in annual installments.

tem (unlike the New Panchayat System which we will describe later) brought about no change in the institution of the headman acting as Police Patel. Under the old *panchayat* system the Police Patel was the chairman of the village *panchayat* and retained in his person the authority associated with the office of headman. In this traditional form of self-government we may see the survival of a primitive institution—that of having a hereditary chief of the village.

Village Self-Government under the Panchayat System

After Indian independence, the Kingdom of Baroda was made a part of Bombay State, and under the Bombay State Panchayat Act of 1952 the New Panchayat System was put into effect in the surveyed area. As we have already noted, Gokulpura was originally a colony of the village of Bahili, and since, under the new requirements, it did not have sufficient population to organize a *panchayat* of its own, it was combined with Samiala under the Samiala village *panchayat*. Not only did this institution differ from the traditional organization of village self-government, but as a result of its implementation, two villages which hitherto had had no connection with each other except that of propinquity came to share a common political organization.

The *panchayat* system instituted in Bombay State differs in some respects from that put into effect in Gujarat State, which superseded Bombay State in 1959. We shall describe the present situation in the surveyed area. The members of the *panchayat* are elected from two constituencies representing Samiala and Laximipura and from one constituency which includes Gokulpura. Three members are elected by each constituency, and the total membership of the *panchayat* is nine. These must include three members who represent the scheduled castes, including the untouchables and the tribal peoples, and the women of the villages. Although in theory an elected assembly, in fact, no general elections have been held for the Samiala village *panchayat*. The present *panchayat* has been made up by the influential members of the castes and residential districts choosing the persons they wish to represent them and then adjusting the number of representatives to fit the established number of *panchayat* members. These people thus become members of the *panchayat* without any electoral contest.

After the chosen *panchayat* members have been recognized by a body called the Local Board, which is a part of the District administration, they become a properly constituted *panchayat*. They choose from among themselves a *sarpanch* and a deputy *sarpanch*. The *sarpanch* may be described as the chairman of the *panchayat*, and at the same time he is the headman of the village. At the present time, the Police Patel system is still in existence, and the *sarpanch* still assists in the collection of taxes and sends in the monthly register of births and deaths. However, there has been a large-scale transfer of the powers relating to village self-government from the Police Patel to the *sarpanch*, and the office of Police Patel will be abolished in the near future.

The *panchayat* employs a clerk to handle the mechanics of village administration and a messenger to run errands, clean out the village office, and perform other services. The clerk is a Brahmin who had been a *talati*, and who had been living in retirement in Baroda. At one time he not only held the post of clerk to the Samiala *panchayat*, but acted in the same capacity for the *panchayat* of three neighboring villages as well. However, the administrative system was changed at the end of October 1962, and the present arrangement is that the Government appoints the *talati* and makes him official clerk to the *panchayat* at the same time. This paves the way for the administration of tax-collection through the *panchayat* rather than through the Police Patel. The former clerk, in light of his experience as an employee of the village, assists the *talati* and official clerk of the *panchayat* in tax-collection, and he undertakes the necessary work in the four villages in which he formerly served.[7] The *sarpanch*, assisted by these clerks, draws up a budget and statement of accounts, and these are debated by the *panchayat*, prior to

[7] It is arranged that the *talati* and official clerk of the *panchayat* shall be in Samiala from Monday to Thursday and in Gokulpura on Friday and Saturday. However, the person in question, who lives in Baroda, does not come to the villages unless there is some business for him to deal with. His salary has been increased by his being appointed official clerk to the *panchayat*, and he must frequently present himself at the office of the Mamlatdar of Baroda Thalka (the head official of the *thalka* administration). The former clerk is principally employed in the office-work connected with tax-collection in the villages, receiving a fixed salary of Rs 20 per month and a "dearness allowance" of Rs 10. He, too, does not come to the village except when there is work for him to do. The messenger receives a salary of Rs 10, and it goes without saying that the post is not a hereditary one. The present messenger is a Baria.

approval by the *gram saba*. Under the old system there were arrangements for the collection of funds for village expenditures, but under the New Panchayat System 30 per cent of the land revenue is alloted to the village, and the *panchayat* is also empowered to levy village rates in accordance with defined conditions. All increases in these village rates must receive the approval of the people of the village. However, the *gram saba* is poorly attended when it is convened for such purposes,[8] and its actual function is only that of giving approval to the decisions which have been arrived at by the *gram agewan*.

As superior organs to these village *panchayats* there are *thalka panchayats*, and above them the Local Board of the District, which is also called the *zilla panchayat*. However, these superior organs are not yet performing all their functions, and the *zilla panchayat* (consisting of representatives of the 120 or so villages in the District, one representative being appointed for about every 10 villages) has been organized only for the purpose of giving formal approval to the budgets passed by the village *panchayats*. A judicial *panchayat* called the *naya panchayat* has also come into being under the New Panchayat System. This body deals with disputes which are not of so serious a nature as to require legal proceedings in court. In Samiala it appears that the two persons selected for the *naya panchayat* were able, in consultation with influential people in the village, to bring about the settlement of a dispute which had arisen in the village. This *naya panchayat* is composed of ten members representing five other villages in the neighborhood as well as Samiala.[9] At present Samiala is represented in this body by only one member—A. Patel, a rich peasant of Gokulpura.

In order to arrive at a better understanding of the activities of the village *panchayat*, let us first give an account of the village

[8] The *gram saba* is supposed to be a village assembly and, as such, should include all the people living in the village, but the figures for attendance of the budget meeting of *gram saba* in the last three years show that only a few persons were present—31 in 1959, 25 in 1960, and 15 in 1961.

[9] The two former members of the *naya panchayat* were the Sadu Brahmin of the Radhakrishna Temple, and one of the leaders of the Muslims who had served a term as deputy *sarpanch*. It was during their term of service that the dispute between two of the villagers was settled. Fines were imposed and paid into the *panchayat* treasury. The present member was chosen by the village *panchayat* in September 1962, but there has been no meeting of the *naya panchayat* sinec that time.

finances in recent years. Tables 5 and 6 give the figures for the fiscal years 1961–62 and 1962–63 as well as those for the two fiscal years which preceded them.

TABLE 5. Panchayat Income

	1962–63	1961–62	1960–61	1959–60
1. House Rate	911.75	664.25	967.50	723.25
2. Hotel and Shop Rate	82.00	57.00	120.00	73.00
3. Factory Rate	57.50	25.00	67.50	—
4. Water Rate	858.07	624.00	1,025.50	400.12
5. Rent from Land	18.00	—	—	—
6. 30% of Land Revenue	2,500.00	3,000.00	2,162.49	2,072.48
7. Interest	706.69	100.00	231.07	81.40
Total	5,134.01	4,470.25	4,574.06	3,350.25
Brought Forward	2,000.00	3,450.00	4,893.41	3,664.41
Grand Total	7,134.01	7,920.25	9,467.47	7,014.66

The accounting year runs from April to March. The budget is made up at the end of December.

As we can see in Table 5, the income of the village of Samiala as a unit of local government comprising almost 350 families (including the houses near the railway station) is, annually, about Rs 5,000. This is equivalent to an income of Rs 15 from each family. The largest item of income is the grant of 30 per cent of the land revenue. The next largest item of income is the house rate, which is levied at Rs .25 per Rs 100 assessed value. There are about 500 houses in the village, of which about fifteen are exempted from the house rate. The valuation is made by the *panchayat*, and this has resulted in relatively low assessments for large and splendid houses, while a heavy tax-burden is imposed on the roughly constructed houses in which the poor villagers live. The water rate is paid for the water raised from the electric-pump well and thus is paid only by the inhabitants of the main agglomeration of Samiala. This rate is set in four grades schematically laid down according to the number of persons in the household, and we may be justified in thinking that it is an excessive burden on the lower strata of the village community. The hotel and shop rate is collected from a small, shack-like teashop which has been set up by the roadside and from a number of very poor shops—six in Samiala and two in Gokulpura—including general stores, greengrocers, milk sellers, and cotton merchants. The factory rate is levied from a ginning factory near the station which operates between January and March. Lastly, the interest income comes from the Central Co-operative Bank, in which all the *panchayat* funds are invested with the exception of a sum of Rs 100 which the *sarpanch* keeps at hand.

TABLE 6.   Panchayat Expenditure

Running Expenses	1962–63	1961–62	1960–61	1959–60
Common Expenditure for Work				
1. Clerk and Messenger	480.00	480.00	480.00	480.00
2. Travel Allowances				
Clerk	100.00	100.00	99.50	81.74
Panchayat Members	50.00	50.00	—	—
3. Contingency Fund	120.00	120.00	113.30	107.56
Waterworks				
4. Electricity	300.00	300.00	264.58	247.79
5. Repairs	500.00	500.00	327.75	498.12
6. General Fund	50.00	100.00	—	—
7. Servant	180.00	182.44	127.75	174.00
8. Water Rate Refund	—	—	0.10	1.75
9. Stand Posts (Taps)	—	—	250.00	—
Tanks				
10. Tanks in Samiala	200.00	200.00	—	64.25
11. Tanks in Laximipura	—	—	—	192.42
Wells				
12. Wells in Laximipura	250.00	250.00	—	—
Roads				
13. Road to Well for Cattle	900.00	1,247.00	—	—
14. Drainage Channels	100.00	300.00	—	—
15. Road Reconstruction	150.00	250.00	163.50	—
Health and Hygiene				
16. Two Bhangi Streetcleaners	240.00	240.00	204.00	204.00
(Samiala and Gokulpura)				
17. Sweeper	10.00	10.00	5.06	4.56
18. Cleaning of Tanks	25.00	25.00	20.00	20.00
Electricity				
19. Electric Fittings	1,850.00	47.56	—	—
Panchayat Office				
20. Painting and Repairs	100.00	200.00	—	—
Education				
21. Building two rooms in	—	1,953.00	—	—
Gokulpura School				
Village Welfare				
22. Number Plates for Houses	300.00	300.00	—	—

Extras

23. Extra Expenditure on Radios (Samiala and Gokulpura)	120.00	120.00	120.00	—
24. Libraries	45.00	45.00	30.00	30.00
25. Special Expenditure on Religious Books	50.00	27.00	—	—
26. Festival Celebrations	50.00	50.00	37.00	15.12
27. Assistance in Case of Accident	150.00	150.00	—	—
28. House Rate Refund	—	—	0.50	—
29. Rural Development Fund	228.63	167.52	243.62	—
Total	6,548.63	7,414.52	2,486.57	2,121.25
Brought Forward	585.38	505.73	6,980.90	4,893.41
Grand Total	7,134.01	7,920.25	9,467.47	7,014.66

Let us now look at the expenditure side of the accounts. As we have noted, the salaries paid to the clerk and the messenger are Rs 30 for the clerk and Rs 10 for the messenger per month. The expenditure on water works is treated as a separate item in the accounts because it concerns only the main agglomeration of Samiala. We may note that the expenditures under this head exceed the income from the water rate. The item "stand posts" in the 1960–61 accounts represents the expense incurred in setting up two water taps in the untouchable quarter of the village. The expense incurred for the well at Laximipura was for an iron railing to make it easier to draw water from the well. The expenditure for the "road to well for cattle" was for the repair of the road from the main village of Samiala to the drinking-place used every day by the oxen and water-buffaloes of the village. The salaries listed under health and hygiene include a salary of Rs 12 per month paid to a Bhangi of Samiala, and one of Rs 5 per month paid to a Bhangi of Gokulpura; in return the two Bhangis are required to clean their villages once a week. The expenditure under electricity was for the installation of street lighting. The 1961–62 expenditure was incurred in nego- tiations and planning, and the street lights are to come into use in the near future. The expense of the construction of two classrooms was incurred on behalf of the Gokulpura Primary School, which is conducted in the communal lodging-house or *darmasara*, as is com- mon in the villages of this area. The inhabitants of Gokulpura sub- scribed a sum equal to that promised by the *panchayat*, and the Government gave a subsidy equal to the total of Rs 3,906 thus con-

situated. It may seem a little strange that the expenditure for providing number-plates for houses should appear under the head of village welfare, but as a result of this measure each family now has a number, and these numbers are used in the electoral roll and other such documents. From the expenditure listed for libraries we might suppose that a fairly large collection of books would be available for the villagers' use, but the libraries consist of only a few small, roughly made book cases set up in a corner of one of the primary school classrooms. Under this head Rs 30 is disbursed on behalf of Samiala and Rs 15 on behalf of Gokulpura. In this matter too, Laximipura is ignored. The expenses incurred in the celebration of festivals were for the celebration in the name of the *pancha-yat* of the anniversary of the establishment of the Republic on January 26, Independence Day on August 15, and the New Year in October. Lastly, the item "rural development fund" represents the village contribution to the development program which is being carried out in this area.

The concerns of village self-government as carried on by the *panchayat* may be roughly inferred from these accounts of income and expenditure. We shall now go on to give a more detailed description of the manner in which the business of the *panchayat* is actually carried on.

The office of the Samiala village *panchayat*, as is shown on the map, is a building located in the square in front of the two temples. The doorless, verandah-like hall is furnished with tables and chairs, and is used for meetings. Documents are kept in a case in the room on the left, which is also used as a place for cooking when the Brahmin clerk is in the office. In the room on the right there is a battery radio fitted into a bookcase, and it is possible to speak to the villagers over loudspeakers fitted up outside. The files kept in the case of documents include the *Record of V. P. Meetings (Information and Decisions), Details of Income and Expenditure of the V.P., Monthly Reports of Income and Expenditure, Registration of Houses and Land, Tax Records of Shops and Factories, Tax Records of Houses, Tax Records of Water Rates, Tax-Collection Books (House and Water Rates), Receipts for Houses, Water and Shop Rates, Other Receipts,* etc. Only the Gujarat language is used in these files, and the numerals are also written in the Gujarat script. The files used in levying the village rates cannot be described as efficient. Besides these, there is the land revenue register kept by the *talati*, but it is difficult to use because the various plots of land owned by any one individual are not listed in one place. There is no village domiciliary register, nor any system under which inhabitants of the village are required to register themselves. This makes it very difficult to conduct a survey of the village.

If we consult the record of business of the *panchayat* we will be able to get some idea of the matters with which it deals and the frequency of its meetings. The *panchayat* met seventeen times in the period between January 1962 and January 1963. These meetings were called after the *panchayat* messenger had gone round the houses of the members with an "information book" in which the subject of discussion had been written and against which each of the members had to sign his name. This was done a few days before the scheduled meeting. It appears that none of these meetings was adjourned for lack of a quorum, but it was rare for every member to be present. The attendance rate of the scheduled caste members and of the female member was poorer than that of the other members. On the rare occasions when she did attend, the female member had very little to say. The scheduled caste members seem to have taken part in the discussions with more frequency than the female member, but in general the business of the *panchayat* was carried on by the influential members, led by the *sarpanch*, and it was they who arrived at the decisions which were taken by the *panchayat*.

Antagonisms and Conflicts in Village Self-Government

When the New Panchayat System came into effect in 1952, the majority of the influential citizens of Samiala were not interested in it. At the same time, the Patidars of Gokulpura were aggrieved at the prospect of forming a *panchayat* with Samiala, and in order to make clear their opposition they refused to put forward any of their members as candidates for membership of the new institution.

It was in such an atmosphere that the able and purposeful D. S. Patel organized the first *panchayat* (Table 7) and took the post of *sarpanch*. The Sadu Brahmin of the Radhakrishna Temple was chosen as deputy *sarpanch*. Patel, who was then 35, got an able young man from the Barias, P. Gohil (24), and one of the leaders of the Muslims, G. Sayad (36), to join him as members of the *panchayat*. None of the other Patidars was included in the new *panchayat*. Under the leadership of the enterprising and eloquent

TABLE 7.   Members of the First Panchayat

Name	Caste	Occupation	Land Holding	Notes
D. S. Patel	Patidar	Agriculture	3.8	Sarpanch
G. H. Vaidya	Brahmin	Priest	—	Deputy Sarpanch
P. B. Gohil	Baria	Agriculture	2.8	
M. N. Padhiar	Baria	Agriculture	1.3	
G. J. Sayad	Muslim	Agriculture	4.1	
U. R. Baria	Kacchia	Housewife	—	Female Member
K. J. Sadu	Vankar	Priest	—	Scheduled

Patel, the first *panchayat* set about the tasks of village government with the vigor of youth, and by 1954 it was making plans for laying on a piped water supply. The *panchayat* encountered some measure of opposition among the villagers, some of whom did not wish to pay a water rate, but the plans went forward. In 1955 the loud-speaker apparatus was installed in the *panchayat* office. Towards the end of the first *panchayat*'s four year term, plans were made for the installation of electric light in private houses, although this was not undertaken by the *panchayat* itself. Patel, using his abilities and enjoying a dictatorial position, gained self-confidence. He is said to have boasted that no one could overthrow his control of the village.

In November 1956, when the re-election of the *panchayat* was impending, Patel presented to the District Office a list of candidates which included his wife as the female member. He did this without consulting any of the people of Samiala. He had made his intentions known to his intimates, and he had also gone to Gokulpura (which he had boycotted until then) where he asked influential members of the Patidar caste to take part in the *panchayat* and succeeded in inducing A. M. Patel to serve as deputy *sarpanch*. After reaching an agreement, Patel and his supporters went in a body to pay their electoral deposits of Rs 15, and then announced the forthcoming election to the villagers. By that time the closing date for candidacy in the election had passed. It was Patel's expectation that, if the election outcome was seen to be determined in advance, the villagers would accept it with philosophical resignation, and that thereafter his personal power would enable him to get his own way. However, Patel's expectations were too optimistic; his political maneuvers resulted in a strengthening of the group opposed

to him and a widespread misunderstanding of his motives, which
produced no small degree of ill-feeling.

TABLE 8.   Members of the Second Panchayat

Name	Caste	Village	Occupation	Land Holding	Notes
D. S. Patel	Patidar	Samiala	Agriculture	3.8	Sarpanch
A. M. Patel	Patidar	Gokulpura	Agriculture	5.0	Deputy Sarpanch
M. I. Patel	Patidar	Samiala	Agriculture	2.8	
M. J. Patel	Patidar	Gokulpura	Agriculture	6.9	
P. B. Gohil	Baria	Samiala	Agriculture	2.8	
G. J. Sayad	Muslim	Samiala	Agriculture	4.1	
M. K. Vassawa	Bhil	Samiala	Postman	—	Scheduled
P. P. Patel	Patidar	Samiala	Housewife	—	Female Member
J. A. Rathod	Rathod	Samiala	Valtania	—	Scheduled

The trouble arose over Patel's determination to push through his
plan for the installation of an electric-pump water system. Some of
the influential members of the community who were in the *panchayat* were more anxious to have petrol lamps for street-lighting,
and most of them, being careful with money, were disinclined to pay
a water rate. The old ruling class of Patidars also reacted against
the young Patel's dictatorial methods. Most of the Barias believed
that the arrest of one of their members by the police on a charge of
illicitly manufacturing alcoholic liquors was the result of information given by Patel and D. G. Sayad. The behavior of these two
was demonstrated when Patel saw a drunk man of the Bhil caste
making himself a nuisance to the villagers; he informed G. Sayad,
who beat the man until he bled.

Again, the Brahmin who had been deputy *sarpanch* in the first
panchayat retained much of his authority after he relinquished his
post. Although he did not attend the meetings of the *panchayat*
regularly, he had a clash with Patel over the fact that he had built
a little wooden hut inside the temple and had put a man in it as a
small shopkeeper. Patel maintained that the shop should be subject
to the shop rate, but the Brahmin resisted the idea until in the end
he was told that if he was not prepared to pay the shop rate, he
would have to close the shop and the shop was closed. The Brahmin
also began to maneuver and got the reputable and trustworthy P. J.
Patel to organize a village petition which was sent up to the District
Office. J. Shah of the Bania caste also lent his assistance. When the

petition was presented, the District Office ordered that a second election be held, and it was held three months later.

The counteractivities of P. J. Patel and his supporters had the desired effect. About two-thirds of the Patidars and the greater part of the village's influential citizens were members of P. J. Patel's party. The majority of the Barias also became "anti-D. Patel." The controlling influence of G. Sayad kept about three-quarters of the Muslims on D. S. Patel's side, but the greater part of the lower castes and the untouchables followed the P. J. Patel group. Patel and Sayad lost their chance of being nominated for the *panchayat*, and even if they had contested the election, their chances of being elected would have been greatly reduced. However, the Patidars of Gokulpura were so disillusioned by the sectarian squabbles of Samiala that they decided not to put forward any of their number as candidates for the *panchayat*; and D. Patel and G. Sayad took advantage of the situation and became members of the *panchayat* by standing as candidates for Gokulpura.

P. J. Patel, who became the *sarpanch* of the third *panchayat*, was firmly opposed to the plans brought forward by the previous *panchayat*. The plans for the water system, on which work had just begun, were carried through but the plan to install electric lights was set aside. P. Patel explained to those who had applied for electricity that it was dangerous and might burn down their houses, and so the village remained unlit. It appears that there was considerable antagonism between the two factions in the village at this time, and the villagers still remember how the two Patels argued so furiously in the village square that it was feared they might come to blows. Even with their absolute majority in the *panchayat*, however, P. Patel's party could not afford to ignore D. Patel, with his abounding energy and his grasp of the functions of the *panchayat*. With the passage of time, feelings of antagonism towards D. Patel became less intense. The waterworks, to which there had been so much opposition, were found, on completion, to be very useful, and the value of D. Patel's work was reappraised. The conservative P. Patel is an impulsive man, and it was because of his impulsiveness that he became the leader of the opposition to D. Patel, but he is fundamentally a quiet man, and as time has passed, it has become more rare for him to engage in open conflict. Meanwhile, D. Patel had found new scope for his abilities; in 1959 he had recovered sufficient power to organize the Agricultural Co-operative Association.

TABLE 9. Members of the Third Panchayat

Name	Caste	Village	Occupation	Land Holding	Notes
P. J. Patel	Patidar	Samiala	Agriculture	4.6	Sarpanch
M. S. Padhiar	Baria	Samiala	Agriculture	1.8	Deputy Sarpanch
C. H. Baria	Baria	Samiala	Agriculture	0.7	
M. K. Sayad	Muslim	Samiala	Agriculture	3.5	
D. S. Patel	Patidar	Samiala	Agriculture	3.8	
G. J. Sayad	Muslim	Samiala	Agriculture	4.1	
M. K. Bhil	Bhil	Samiala	Day Laborer	—	Scheduled
H. R. Bhangi	Bhangi	Gokulpura	Sweeper	—	Scheduled

The election of the fourth *panchayat* fell due in 1962, but the *panchayat* was again chosen by nomination and not by an electoral contest. P. Patel left the *panchayat*, but both D. Patel and G. Sayad were included in it. The name of P. Gohil, who was chosen by Patel as one of the members of the first *panchayat*, again appeared in the list of members. This might lead us to believe that D. Patel had triumphed over the old ruling class represented by P. Patel and had re-established himself, but this was not so. The *panchayat* included P. Patel's wife, J. P. Patel, as the female member, and the Patidars of Gokulpura, finding it inconvenient not to have a representative in the *panchayat*, nominated the young N. Patel and his wife. There was also one member from the village of Laximipura. Those members who come from outside the main village of Samiala have felt some degree of antipathy toward it, and while they recognize D. Patel's ability, they are critical of his dictatorial methods.

TABLE 10. Members of the Fourth Panchayat

Name	Caste	Village	Occupation	Land Holding	Notes
P. B. Gohil	Baria	Samiala	Agriculture	2.8	Sarpanch
D. S. Patel	Patidar	Samiala	Agriculture	4.5	Deputy Sarpanch
N. M. Patel	Patidar	Gokulpura	Agriculture	3.5	
K. J. Parmar	Baria	Gokulpura	Agriculture	0.4	
S. B. Padhiar	Baria	Laximipura	Agriculture	0.7	
G. J. Sayad	Muslim	Samiala	Agriculture	4.1	
L. S. Vankar	Vankar	Samiala	Day Laborer	—	Scheduled
L. N. Patel	Patidar	Gokulpura	Housewife	—	Female Member
J. P. Patel	Patidar	Samiala	Housewife	—	Female Member

For these reasons D. Patel was unable to take up the post of *sarpanch*, and was obliged to give it to P. Gohil. The latter's assumption of the office is a historical event in the village, representing the overthrow of the Patidars' hitherto unshaken ruling position. The majority of the people of the Baria caste, comprising more than 100 families, rejoice in their hearts that this event has taken place. In Gokulpura, where the rule of the Patidars remains unshaken, P. Gohil is better thought of than D. Patel; they feel that they now have a *sarpanch* on whose services they can call and before whom they can frankly state their demands. The present *sarpanch* thus presides over a balance of forces and performs his functions by means of negotiation and compromise.

There are, however, still problems in the Samiala village *panchayat*. Here we may discuss two points. First, under the new system members representing the scheduled castes are included in the *panchayat*, but these members are day-laborers or service workers dependent on the village community who own no land and who have only nominal membership in the *panchayat*. They are still members of the governed, not the governing, class. One concrete example of this is the Samiala water system. Even when the water-taps had been set up, the untouchables were not allowed to use them, and it took another year for lead pipes to be laid to their quarter of the village and for taps to be set up for their special use. Even this was not done in response to their demands, but rather in the face of their poverty-generated opposition. The *panchayat* installed the pipes and taps as planned and, when the untouchables announced their intention of refusing to use the piped water, informed them that it would levy the water rate from them whether they used the water or not. Thus the *panchayat*'s decision made inevitable the untouchables' use of a more convenient form of water supply.

The second problem is Gokulpura's persistent tendency to break away from Samiala. The inhabitants of Gokulpura have not renounced their independent bent, and they are continually expressing their grievances in communications addressed to various bodies. The New Panchayat System requires villages with less than 500 inhabitants to form a *panchayat* in association with neighboring villages, a not unnatural stipulation since small villages do not have the financial resources for all the institutions of government.

However, villagers who have been carrying on local government in
a closed village community feel that such an associated government
is scarcely to be borne. The Patidars of Gokulpura have a lively
consciousness of their membership in their village community and
they are proud of the fact that their village is richer than Samiala.
They feel sad at the prospect of being subordinated to Samiala, a
village which they despise to some extent. Consequently they have
no desire to join with the citizens of Samiala to build up a new unit
of government, Samiala village. These two problems may prove to
be obstacles to the future development of the village *panchayat*.

IV. CHANGES IN VILLAGE ORGANIZATION

Social Change in the Village Community
    The social cohesion of the castes in the surveyed village has de-
creased, and, in particular, class distinction between the members
of different castes has become less conspicuous than in former times.
The untouchables of the lowest castes are still separated from the
rest of the community by a line which can scarcely ever be crossed,
but in the strata above them class distinctions have become almost
imperceptible in the course of daily life.
    In the past, there was a clear distinction between the Patidars and
other high caste families on the one hand and the remainder of the
community on the other. If we look at the land register, we will see
that no surnames are given for persons belonging to castes inferior
to the Patidars.[10]
    It is said that forty or fifty years ago even the Patidars could not
sit down with Brahmins. Caste differences between the Patidars
and the Barias have lessened over the years. The fact that some of
the Barias call themselves Rajputs is not unconnected with a rise
in their relative social position. A singing club called the *bhajan
mandal*, in which religious music is sung in unison to the accom-
paniment of drums and bells, has been organized in a manner which
cuts across caste distinctions. Members of such clubs invite one
another to meetings held in the different villages, at which their

---

[10] It is said that an interest in surnames first penetrated to the lower castes
four and a half centuries ago. It is also common for members of the lower castes
to use the caste name as their surname, but it is not possible to tell a man's caste
by his surname in every case.

music is performed and refreshments served. The taboo on "inter-dining" is cheerfully broken on these occasions. The same is true of the occasions on which tea is served at meetings of the *panchayat*. The latter is an officially convened meeting, and refusal to partake on the grounds of the taboo on "inter-dining" would constitute a criminal offence which might lead to court proceedings; but in the case of the *bhajan mandal* the act is purely voluntary, and if the commensality rules reflecting the hierarchy of the castes were strictly applied, such conduct would be impossible. The women have also organized an inter-caste Women's Association (albeit with the encouragement of an extension worker from the Rural Development Program), and they hold displays of home crafts and cookery as well as meetings every day at an appointed time to sing religious songs in the village temple.[11]

This breaking-up of the barriers between the castes is not un-related to the secularization of village life. The recreational aspect of the *bhajan mandal* is more significant than the religious, and not only religious but also secular music is performed. For this reason, Muslims are also included in the club. Again, the Brahmins and the Gosains say that, in the normal course of events, the villagers do not worship at the temples very frequently. The officiating priests are probably not exaggerating when they lament the lack of religious faith among the villagers. Nevertheless, in both Samiala and Gokulpura the entire village community continues to partici-pate in religious festivals, of which there are about ten at different times throughout the year. In this sense the villagers are still reli-gious, and at these festivals there is little sign of class distinction between the castes, apart from the discrimination against the lowest castes of the village community.[12] The festivals themselves are or-ganized in a manner which provides ample opportunity for re-creational amusement.

The relaxation of class distinctions among the castes and the ten-

[11] The Women's Association of Samiala is led by three women of the Patidar, Baria, and Bhil castes. About 25 women assemble in the temple on three oc-casions every month. The women are generally conservative, and when food is served, the various castes eat at some distance from one another.

[12] In Gokulpura, where the authority of the dominant caste, the Patidars, is still strong, the rule that the castes must eat at some distance from one another is observed when tea and food are served at the Diwari festival and other similar occasions.

dency towards secularization of the life of the villagers have resulted in a weakening of the traditional power of the old ruling class, a theocratic power which presupposed the unity of religious and political institutions. The social effects of this development are all the more decisive when the power of the dominant caste is undermined by changes in the material basis of their power, that is, by changes in land ownership. No such undermining of the power of the Patidars has occurred in Gokulpura, and their dominant position remains unshaken. Further, Gokulpura retains more vestiges of the traditional mechanisms of village self-government than does Samiala, and the difference does not arise solely from the fact that there is no *panchayat* office in Gokulpura and that the village must undertake its own administration. In contrast, changes in the composition of the ruling class are clearly apparent in Samiala.

Under the old system of village self-government the influential members of the Patidar caste, headed by the *matadars*, were able to strengthen their secular authority with the authority which they derived from the performance of religious functions. It was their custom, whenever they punished some minor offence in the village, to present a quantity of grain to a "pigeon tower." There are no towers of this kind in Gokulpura, but in many of the villages in this region a pigeon tower is located in the center of the village. These towers have been built by influential Patidars in order to demonstrate the sincerity of their religious faith. In Samiala there is a Pigeon Tower and Dog Association. To this association two Patidars each donated 0.8 hectares of land, and a Bania 0.4 hectares of land. This land is cultivated by M. Patel, a son of one of the donors. M. Patel is one of the village elders who served as Police Patel several times. From the income which he makes from the land, he deducts Rs 125 for costs and entrusts the remainder to the management of J. Shah, who is a grandson of one of the donors. This money enables M. Patel to provide food for the pigeons every day between June and September. He also distributes 100 kg of grain every year among a number of dog-troughs which his father established at several places in the village. We may suppose that in times past these activities endowed the Patidars and Banias with authority in the eyes of the religiously-minded villagers. Members of the leading families also contributed to the expenses of the festivals and presided at the ceremonies performed in the course of them. The family of

A Zamindar's Mansion (West Bengal)

Cow Dung on a Farmhouse Wall (West Bengal)

Building a Mud House   (West Bengal)

Barber and Village Headman   (West Bengal)

M. Patel is accustomed to celebrating religious festivals on its own account and to distributing food to the villagers.

However, such religious practices have lost much of their emotional appeal among the secularized villagers of the present day. The power of the old Patidar dominant group has been weakened by a decrease in the number of Patidar families and by the fact that their economic pre-eminence has been destroyed. It is this situation which gave D. S. Patel, who is not a member of a *matadar* family, the opportunity to come forward as an able leader of a new type, and the New Panchayat System has raised him to the top of a new influential group. Not only does he command the support of a section of the Patidars, but he has also secured an alliance with the leaders of the Muslims, and is extending his influence over the Baria caste as well. He is thus a man of a character different from the members of the old *matadar*-led group.

We may say that this change is a change from the principle of hereditary rule to the principle of tenure of office on the basis of ability. Patel's overconfidence led him to make the mistake of attempting a forceful dictatorship, but in Samiala, where socio-economic changes have been taking place in the village community, the failure of his first efforts was not fatal, and he has not fallen from power. His personality has caused him to be misunderstood and mistrusted, but he has rebuilt the basis of his power by his organization of the Agricultural Co-operative Association. The allegiance of the villagers can no longer be commanded by leaders whose only policy is the maintenance of the *status quo*, and the village can no longer be ruled by the Patidars alone.

Although it is not yet very active, the Agricultural Co-operative Association deals in fertilizers, lends money, and markets cotton. It thus comes into competition with the cotton merchants, the most important being J. Shah of the Bania caste and one of the Patidars. The existence in the background of such conflicts of interest colors the dynamics of village self-government. J. Shah of the Bania caste is one of the hidden leaders in the village, and is allied with the old ruling group of Patidars.

The social dynamics of village self-government which we have described will probably persist in the future. It is impossible to prophesy in what manner they will develop, but it is clear that there can be no return to the old order of village government. This is also true of Gokulpura, where the socio-economic organization has not undergone much change. There is still a great disparity between the power of the Patidars and that of the Barias in the village, but the times will not allow the Patidars to rule alone. The leaders in that village are no longer the Police Patel and the great landowners, but men like the advanced peasant A. Patel and the notably able N. Patel, who was recently elected to the *panchayat*. Thus, in Gokulpura as in Samiala, we can discern a transition from the principle of hereditary rule to the principle of tenure of office on the basis of ability.

Change and Stagnation in the Village Community

As the analyses presented in the preceding pages show, the surveyed village has undergone many changes. We may well suppose that there is considerable difference between the present village organization and that of half a century ago. These changes have been particularly marked in the period since independence.

Modern agriculture includes the use of commercial fertilizers and the employment of electric pumps for the water system. The *jajmani* system which characterized the self-sufficient economy of the Indian village has almost disappeared. The milk which the villagers produce is collected every day by the agents of a factory in Baroda and is transported to that city by bicycle. Baroda market is still held once a week, and now that there is a frequent bus service it is an everyday occurrence for the villagers to make purchases in the city. The villagers thus find themselves in need of ready cash, and not a few of them have sought work in Baroda or in the vicinity. There has also been an increase in the quantity of cash crops, and there is a larger number of peasants who are specializing in vegetable production. The economic organization of the village could not but change, and these economic changes have affected the village organization.

Further, as we have already described in detail, the new system of political administration has broken up the old order of village self-government. The land reform, although it was a half-hearted measure with many loopholes, had considerable effect on the village, especially since some of the village land was owned by absentee landlords living in Baroda. The provisions of the Tenancy Law are bringing about changes in the conditions of land-tenancy.

The Rural Development Program organized by the national and state governments has also exercised some influence on the village. Experimental activities in the sphere of social education which are being carried on by the Social Education Organization Training Center are also having their effect.

The Kingdom of Baroda gave much attention to education, and thanks to the tradition thus established, the present villagers enjoy a fair level of education. As can be seen in Table 11, the level of education among the middle and lower strata of the village is lower than that of the Patidars and there are many persons who have had no education at all, but the present situation is a great advance over the days when literacy was entirely confined to the upper stratum. As the development of communications and the break-down of the closed self-sufficient village economy have brought the villagers into closer contact with the city, they have become more modernized. This process of urbanization has proceeded alongside the changes which have taken place in the traditional village community.

TABLE 11.   Number of Years of Education Received by Men and Women Over 21 Years of Age

| Caste | | Years of Education | | Total Number |
	0	1—3	4 or more	of Persons
Brahmin	1	1	5	7
Bania	1	—	1	2
Patidar	33	13	82	128
Kacchia	1	4	3	8
Kumbhar	2	7	7	16
Luhor	1	—	2	3
Baria	199	82	78	359
Valand	3	2	3	8
Bhoi	—	2	—	2
Ravalia	5	1	2	8
Rathod	5	1	—	6
Bhil	3	4	3	10
Vaghri	32	2	4	38
Vankar	42	21	19	82
Chamar	2	1	1	4
Bhangi	5	4	4	13
Muslim	57	16	37	110
Total	392	161	251	804

Cases in which the number of years of education received was not known have been omitted.

The forces, however, which have been bringing change to the village community have not brought about any radical alteration in the social organization. Progress in the organization of agriculture is slight, and it needs hardly be said that only members of the upper stratum of society use electric pumps and commercial fertilizers. The villagers who are involved in the exchange of goods with Baroda are also members of this upper stratum. The poor villagers of the lower strata cannot engage in such commerce, and even when they are able to purchase something, they are obliged by lack of ready money to buy on credit at inflated prices from the little retail shops in the village. Although an agricultural co-operative has been started, the poor peasants are obliged to sell their cotton to the cotton merchants because of the debts which they have incurred. We may say, therefore, that the development of a commercial economy has only accelerated the processes of social stratification. Yet in the course of the transition from a self-sufficient economy to a commercial money economy there is the increased possibility of members of the upper stratum coming to ruin and greater opportunities for members of the middle and lower strata to rise in the social scale. The rise in social position of the middle stratum castes which followed the land reform was particularly noticeable.

The members of the lower and lowest strata have not been in possession of the resources necessary to make use of such opportunities for social advancement. We have already described how the Vankars of Samiala have close contacts with the cities and leave the village to go to temporary work in brick factories near Bombay and Surat. As a result, their standard of living is better than that of members of the lower castes and of the more impoverished Barias in the middle stratum of the village community. The part of the village in which they live is also well-kept, and small landowners have appeared among them; but their position in the village as a whole has not been raised. Because of the uncertain nature of their employment outside the village they show no signs of wishing to dissociate themselves completely from the village, but they are still regarded as untouchables in their place of domicile.

We may say, therefore, that changes in the political institutions cannot improve the social conditions of the lower castes, although they have brought about other changes in the village. The provision of seats in the *panchayat* for members of the scheduled castes is a

measure unprecedented in the traditional form of village self-government, but until the members who fill these seats have the necessary economic backing, representation of the scheduled castes will
be merely nominal in the face of the long-standing and persistent
tradition of untouchability in India. Even when class distinctions
among the castes of the upper and middle strata have become imperceptible in daily life, caste distinctions will still be present in the
lives of the members of these strata, in spite of the superficial appearance of equality, so long as they are separated by a strict line of
demarcation from the castes of the lower stratum of society. Activities in social education could not be carried on if these facts were
not recognized. Since the Indian policy of giving privileges to the
scheduled castes in order to raise their social position and do away
with untouchability is not supported by any policy for the improvement of their economic condition, it has had the reverse effect of
maintaining untouchability and drawing attention to its existence.
Untouchability will not disappear unless fundamental changes are
made in the economic bases of society down to village level.

    The village untouchables are allowed to send their children to
the primary school, where attendance is compulsory. The Vankars
of Samiala, having been exposed to the society of the cities, send a
relatively large number of children to the school, and the school attendance rate among them is higher than among the poor people
of the Baria caste. The rate is not as high as that of the Patidars or
the Muslims, nor can they compete with the higher castes in terms
of level of education. It is possible that changes may come about in
this aspect of social life after the construction of factories along the
road to Baroda, in which there will be employment for members of
the lower and lowest strata castes. At the same time, we should
probably not expect too much from this development.

    It is difficult to bring about radical changes in the society of the
Indian village. If by radical change we mean the insignificance of
the caste system and the disappearance of untouchability, then radical change is not possible in Samiala in the foreseeable future. That
is how difficult the problem is.

B) A Village in a Paddy Producing Area

I. A GENERAL DESCRIPTION OF THE VILLAGE

Going north from Calcutta by express train for about two hours,
we arrive at the town of Bolpur, located in Birbhum District in the
state of West Bengal. About 4 km to the northwest lies Santiniketan,
where the poet Tagore founded Visva-Bharati University in 1901.
If we take the road which passes in front of the Bolpur station for
about 5 km to the southwest, turn off to the left and travel another
1.5 km, we will come to Supur village. This was our survey village
in a wet paddy area.

From Bolpur to the point at which we turned off to the left a well-
surfaced road runs through a broad expanse of rice fields. The road
which leads into the village is an uneven, dusty track, and it is so
narrow that motor vehicles can scarcely make their way along it.
There are few buses in this area, and the villagers use ox-carts or
bicycles as their principal means of transport.

TABLE 12.   Area, Number of Households, and Population, 1961

	Supur	Nurpur	Ramchandrapur	Hat Rasulganj	Total
Area (sq. km.)	1.0	2.0	2.2	0.6	5.8
Number of Households	117	164	62	62	405
(1951)	(105)	(174)	(33)	(60)	(372)
Population	579	776	320	327	2,002
(per household)	(4.95)	(4.73)	(5.16)	(5.27)	(4.94)
Male	284	385	165	157	991
Female	295	391	155	176	1,011
Population, 1951	414	784	165	273	1,636
(per household)	(3.94)	(4.50)	(5.00)	(4.55)	(4.40)
Illiterates, 1951	361	685	148	168	1,365
(%)	(87.5)	(87.5)	(89.4)	(61.5)	(83.5)

It would appear that there was a considerable degree of under-reporting in the 1951 census. The
results of the 1961 census are not yet published, but we were able to use the census tables kept at
the Block Development Office.

The surveyed area comprises four *mouja* named Supur, Nurpur,
Ramchandrapur, and Hat Rasulganj. A *mouja* is an administrative

unit of tax-collection. Data in the 1951 and 1961 censuses give a general description of the surveyed area. Figures for number of persons per household are similar to those of Samiala (Table 12), but the illiteracy rate is much higher in Supur. If we look at the distribution of population over the various occupations, as shown in Table 13, we will see that the number of cultivating proprietors is much smaller than in the Gujarat village and that a large proportion of the population is listed as tenant cultivator and agricultural laborer. This may be attributed to the existence in West Bengal State of the Zamindari system, through which the greater part of the peasants had lost their land by the time these census data were collected.

TABLE 13. Number of Persons Employed in Various Occupations
(percentage), 1951

	Supur	Nurpur	Ramchandrapur	Hat Rasulganj	Total
Agriculture					
Land Wholly or	108	156	23	21	308
Mainly Owned	(26.0)	(19.9)	(13.9)	(7.7)	(18.7)
Land Wholly or	54	278	122	140	594
Mainly Tenanted	(13.0)	(35.4)	(74.0)	(51.3)	(36.4)
Agricultural Laborers	87	312	12	112	523
	(21.0)	(39.5)	(7.3)	(41.0)	(32.0)
Non-Cultivating	—	—	—	—	—
Landlords					
Non-Agricultural					
Other Forms of	42	32	2		76
Production	(10.2)	(4.1)	(1.2)		(4.6)
Commerce	4	2			6
	(1.0)	(0.3)			(0.4)
Transport	—	—	—	—	—
Other Services and	119	4	6		129
Miscellaneous	(28.8)	(0.5)	(3.6)		(7.9)

Table 13 indicates also the small number of persons employed in non-agricultural occupations. As we have already pointed out in the case of Samiala, a low non-agricultural population in a Hindu village does not mean that the village is unaffected by social change but, on the contrary, is a sign that the traditional self-sufficient economy and caste system have fallen into decay. In fact, the older form of village organization has disintegrated to a much greater degree in this village than in Samiala.

The surveyed area is divided into four sub-divisions for tax-collection, but for practical purposes it may be regarded as a single village. The villagers themselves refer to the four divisions as "Supur" and think of it as a single village, although they are conscious that they live in a particular *mouja*. The village *panchayat* is divided, so that there would appear to be two administrative units of village government, but in fact they perform their functions as one body. We shall therefore refer to the surveyed area as a whole as "Supur" and shall deal with the whole administrative area in question, with the exception of two villages, Hetiadanga and Hajrabaganj, which are inhabited by the tribal Santal people and located at some distance from the main agglomeration and the camp for refugees from East Bengal. There are no distinct agglomerations in the surveyed area analogous to the villages of Samiala and Gokulpura, and in the following pages we shall treat the four *mouja* and the two *panchayat* areas as one unit, except when there is some particular necessity to do otherwise.

The main part of the village is located in that part of the administrative area where the boundaries of the four *mouja* meet. Outside this central part of the village there are a number of small agglomerations inhabited by the tribal Santal people and the untouchables. Cultivated land surrounds the village, but the main block of cultivated land lies on the northern side of the road from Bolpur. Midway between this road and the village runs a 10m wide irrigation canal built by the state eight years ago. As we carried out our survey after the harvest had been gathered, there was no water in the fields along either side of the canal nor in the canal itself, and oxen were grazing on the wild vegetation which had grown in the fields since the rice had been harvested. Sugar cane had been planted here and there in the paddy fields, but the crop area was so small that it almost escaped notice.

The river Ojoy runs about 2 km south of the village. It is a fairly large river, with a bed 200–300m wide, but does not have much water in the dry winter season. At one time, the area between the river and the village was used for mango orchards or pasture; it is frequently flooded during the rainy season. A large part of this area has been reclaimed by refugees from East Bengal (Pakistan) and is now under cultivation. There are hardly any paddy fields in the area and the crops grown are sugar cane, potatoes, wheat, mustard, and the jute which the refugees brought with them from East Bengal.

The form of the village agglomerations in the West Bengal survey area is different from that of the Gujarat villages. The latter were built beside one or two large ponds, the houses close together, their walls touching. There are a large number of ponds in Supur; the houses are scattered around them, each house standing on its own. It is true that there are a few places where the houses are built relatively close together, so that they present the appearance of a row or street, but a fairly wide space is left between one house-lot and the next. Palm trees, bushes, or grass grow in the space between the houses. Thus, Supur has a population comparable to Samiala, but it is scattered over an area several times larger than the residential area of Samiala.

As in the Gujarat villages, the best houses in Supur are built of brick, but the majority of houses are small huts made of mud-plaster and thatched with straw. They are poorer than those of Samiala and Gokulpura, a reflection of a generally lower standard of living. There are, however, two large brick buildings in the center of the village, and although they are in ruins, their imposing height dominates their surroundings. These two buildings are the former residence and offices of the Majumdar family, the Zamindar.

There are many ruined buildings in the village, buildings of which only the brick walls remain standing and buildings of which only one corner remains. The history of the village lies concealed in these ruins. Several hundred years ago this village was the site of the palace of the ruler of a small kingdom. Later there was a period during which the village was ruled by the Goswamis of the Brahmin caste, who had defended it against external enemies and were granted the land by the Muslim ruler. At the end of the eighteenth century the French introduced the cultivation of indigo and established a dye-works, and after the Anglo-French War the English took it over and continued to run it for some time. A more important fact in the history of the village was its central position in relation to the trade and commerce of the region before the building of the railway in 1859. The important line of communication was the Ojoy river, and Supur, as one of the towns near the river, was the site of a market during this period. It is said that at the height of its prosperity Supur had a population of 13,000, that the Tambulis, a merchant caste, flourished there, and that there were a number of rich merchants living in the town. After the railway was put through, however, commerce and business moved elsewhere, and Supur declined rapidly. The merchants left the village and their magnificent houses fell into ruins. Also, the great outbreaks of malaria which occurred at frequent intervals carried off large numbers of the population and wiped out many families.

The village thus has a checkered history of prosperity and decline. The many old temples which are to be found in the village bear testimony to this history. What is more, from the time when the Zamindari system was first established under British rule until a few years ago, the village was subject to the Zamindars and was reduced to a state of economic debility. This economic inactivity persists even today. It is principally the East Bengal refugees who engage in positive activities in the village, and the majority of the native inhabitants continue a lackadaisical existence.

Our survey showed that the village is made up of a large number of castes (Table 14). We will leave the detailed discussion of caste until later, but we may observe here that more than 30 per cent of the families are the Santals, the tribal people. In Ramchandrapur a certain number of the Santals were omitted from our survey, and the proportion of the Santals in the total population would be much greater if we were to include those living in the two Santal villages in the Nurpur sector of the surveyed area. Excluding the Santals and the Muslims (13 per cent of the households), there is no single caste which includes a large number of households. The village is thus made up of a large number of castes each of which includes only a few households.

We can divide the castes into groups as indicated by the dotted lines in the table. The castes from the top of the table down to the Kayasthas may be regarded as the upper stratum, the castes ranging between the Tambulis and the Vaisha Saha as the middle, the castes between the Sarnakars and the Ranas as the lower, and those below them as the lowest stratum of the society. Here, too, the castes in the lower stratum are scheduled castes. The Baishnabs and Muslims, listed at the end of the table, are not included in the caste ranking. Although the Baishnabs are Hindus, they constitute a special sect. The greater number of the Baishnabs in the village are persons who were Brahmins before they joined the sect, and their social standing is high. All the members of the Kayastha, Vaisha Saha, and Nama Sudra castes are refugees from East Bengal.

TABLE 14. Number of Households in Each Caste in the Various Sectors of the Village

		Supur	Nurpur	Ramchan-drapur	Hat Rasulganj	Total	Per-centage
Brahmin	Priest	3	–	1	–	4	1.2
Rajput Brahmin		–	–	1	–	1	0.3
Baidya	Physician	5	–	–	–	5	1.5
Kayastha		4	6	–	–	10	2.9
Tambuli	Trader	4	3	–	4	11	3.2
Teli	Oil Presser	–	–	–	3	3	0.9
Sadogope	Cultivator	1	3	1	–	5	1.5
Napit	Barber	1	–	–	1	2	0.6
Modok	Sweet-maker	2	2	–	–	4	1.2
Kamar	Blacksmith	–	1	–	–	1	0.3
Shakari	Bangle-maker	5	–	–	–	5	1.5
Vaisha Saha	Trader	3	–	–	1	4	1.2
Sarnakar	Goldsmith	–	3	–	–	3	0.9
Dhopa	Washerman	16	–	–	–	16	4.8
Suri	Wine-maker	3	2	–	–	5	1.5
Goala	Milkman	3	–	–	–	3	0.9
Kolu	Oil-presser	2	–	–	–	2	0.6
Rana	Blacksmith	–	2	1	1	4	1.2
Nama Sudra	Worker	2	2	5	–	9	2.7
Bagdi	Agricultural Worker	23	–	5	–	28	8.5
Kaot	Fisherman	–	1	–	–	1	0.3
Mete	Agricultural Worker	2	–	–	1	3	0.9
Bauri	Agricultural Worker	1	3	–	7	11	3.2
Dome	Basket-maker	1	–	–	1	2	0.6
Hari	Midwife	1	4	–	–	5	1.5
Muchi	Cobbler	4	–	–	1	5	1.5
Bedia Mal	Snake-skin Curer	–	2	–	1	3	0.9
Kora	Tribal	3	–	–	–	3	0.9
Santal	Tribal	24	30	21	42	117	35.0
Muslims		–	44	–	–	44	13.1
Baishnab		6	1	6	2	15	4.4
Total		119	109	41	65	334	100.0

II. The Castes in the Village Community

Caste and the Caste Hierarchy

The caste hierarchy in Supur has disintegrated to a greater degree than in Samiala. In the upper stratum of the scheduled castes
there are some individuals who own land and who have attained
positions of some influence in the village community. However,
there is a clear distinction between the people of the lower castes
and the members of the castes above them, and the superiority of
the higher castes is undeniable. Thus, in the case of Supur as in the
case of Samiala, we must take the caste composition of the village
as basic for our consideration of its organization.

The village contains a large number of castes, as we saw in Table
14. In the table the castes were divided into four groups—the upper,
the middle, the lower, and the lowest.

In Supur, as in Samiala, the Brahmins hold the highest position
in the caste hierarchy. The president of the *panchayat* is a Brahmin,
and the head of a Brahmin household in the Ramchandrapur sector
is a small landlord who also officiates as a priest at the temple
founded by the Goswamis. He is a man of some influence in the village. The third is a poor Brahmin who superintends the distribution
of food to the poor at the Zamindar temple. The remaining Brahmin household is headed by a widow who is related to the president
of the *panchayat*. The Brahmin caste is thus in no position to dominate the village. The Rajput Brahmin household which has come
into the village from Bihar State is not worthy of special consideration.

In the past, the Baidya caste has been the dominant caste in the
village, both in numbers and activity. The Zamindars in the region
belonged either to the Brahmin caste or to the Baidya caste. The
Majumdar family, the Zamindar resident in the village, were
members of the Baidya caste, and the present president of the *panchayat* was their *gomosta*, or tax-collector. The influential families
of the Baidya caste have now left the village, but there are still a
number of Baidya families living there, and as members of the educated class they have a strong voice in village affairs.

The Kayasthas, like the Baidyas, are upper caste, but those living in the village are refugees and as yet do not have much economic power. Some of the more educated have been employed out-

side the village and with the income thus obtained have either bought land or brought new land under cultivation and have embarked upon a new form of agriculture—the cultivation of jute— with hired labor.

Middle stratum castes are known in this region as "the nine castes."

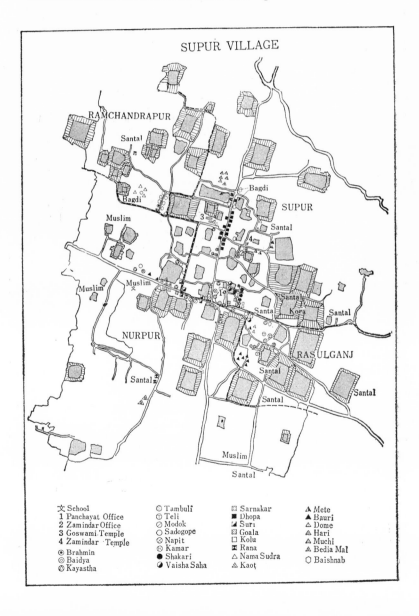

SUPUR VILLAGE

文 School	◎ Tambuli	⊞ Sarnakar	▲ Mete
1 Panchayat Office	⊕ Teli	■ Dhopa	▲ Bauri
2 Zamindar Office	⊘ Modok	◪ Suri	△ Dome
3 Goswami Temple	○ Sadogope	⊠ Goala	△ Hari
4 Zamindar Temple	⊗ Napit	□ Kolu	△ Muchi
◉ Brahmin	⊛ Kamar	⊠ Rana	▲ Bedia Mal
◎ Baidya	● Shakari	△ Nama Sudra	○ Baishnab
◎ Kayastha	◖ Vaisha Saha	▲ Kaot	

They include the Telis (oil-pressers), the Malis (gardeners), the Tambulis, also called Baniks (traders), the Sadogopes (farmers), the Napits (barbers), the Baruis, also called Gochalis (bakers), the Modoks, also called Chites (makers of sweet-meats), the Kumors, also called Pites (potters), and the Kamars (blacksmiths). Six of these castes live in Supur.

As we have already said the Tambuli caste flourished in the village in times past. In those days the village used to hold a market, as is shown by the word *hat* in the name Hat Rasulganj. The innumerable abandoned houses which they left bear testimony to the prosperity of the period, and we may well suppose that the present-day inhabitants are not exaggerating when they say that the Tambulis were powerful enough to stand up to the Baidya Zamindars. Among the Tambulis who remain in the village are some who own large areas of land.

The members of the Teli caste are usually oil-pressers, but they are regarded as traders in Supur. The Sadogope caste are considered the oldest Hindu inhabitants in the region, but the members of the caste living in the village have all moved there recently. The members of one Sadogope household are weavers as well as farmers. The two Napit families moved to the village from East Bengal approximately twenty years ago. It is said that there was a member of the Napit caste living in the village when they arrived, but that his family has since died out. One Modok household still makes sweet-meats. There is only one household of the Kamar caste, and they have abandoned the traditional occupation of blacksmith to become laborers. In addition to the above, the castes represented in the village include the Shakaris, who make the spiral shell bangles used in wedding ceremonies. A caste with a tradition going back to the period of commercial prosperity, there is now only one household engaged in the caste occupation. The four households of the Vaishyas caste are refugees from East Bengal. Starting from nothing, some of them have improved themselves to the extent of being able to buy land and houses.

The castes which rank below those mentioned above may be collectively designated the scheduled castes, but there are certain distinct groups among them, and we must consider them separately. If we divide the scheduled castes into the lower and lowest strata, the castes in the lower strata include the Sarnakars (goldsmiths), the Dhopas (washermen), the Suris (brewers), the Goalas, also called Gopes (milkmen), the Kolus, also called Gorain (oil-pressers), and the Ranas (blacksmiths). The distinction between the ordinary castes and the scheduled castes, which may be made in the case of persons with the same occupation, has come about because some Hindus married the aboriginal population and were expelled from their original castes. For example, the Goala or Gope caste was originally members of the oldest body of Hindu settlers, as were the Sadogope caste, but marrying outside the faith, they lost the right to receive the ministrations of the Brahmins. It is said that the name of the Sadogope caste comes from this distinction—Sadogope signifying "pure and good Gope."

With the exception of one household which owns a shop in Bolpur, the Sarnakars living in the village are employed as laborers. The large number of households belonging to the caste of washermen, the Dhopas, reflects the former commercial prosperity of the village. The members of this caste have now become peasants, and some of them are fairly wealthy. The largest landowner next to the former Zamindar is a Suri, and his household continues its brewing business. The Goalas are farmers, and one of them owns a fair amount of land and is active in village politics. The Kolus are agricultural laborers. Lastly, there are the Ranas, who live near the part of the village inhabited by the Santals. Among them, one household carries on the traditional occupation of blacksmith, and one makes a precarious living as an itinerant merchant.

The castes in the lowest stratum are the untouchables. The Nama Sudras are refugees from East Bengal. The Bagdis are descended from the aboriginal inhabitants of the area, and the majority of them are agricultural laborers. The Kaots are fishermen and the Metes are agricultural laborers. These castes are considered somewhat superior among the lowest castes. Beneath them are ranked the Bauri, Dome, Hari, and Muchi (or Bayen) castes.

The Bauris are said to be a tribal people who came from the south, but half of those living in the village have moved there in the last few years. The Domes are hereditarily basketmakers or drummers but they are also agricultural laborers. The Haris were originally employed as sweepers or pig-breeders. Members of the Dome caste, and also the wives of the Haris, were midwives, and members of the Muchi caste were cobblers, but they are now employed as agricultural laborers or in some similar capacity.

There is also the Bedia Mal caste, whose occupation is skinning snakes and dressing the skins. They are accustomed to burying their own dead, and are regarded as belonging to a lower stratum of society than the untouchables.

Lastly, there are the tribal peoples—the Koras and the Santals. It is said that the Santal tribe moved into this region at the end of the eighteenth century. They are an example of a tribal people who have been Hinduized, but who still retain some of their former customs and ways of living. They are employed as agricultural and non-agricultural laborers.

Outside the hierarchy of castes which we have described, there are also fifteen Baishnab households and almost fifty Muslim households living in the village. As we have already noted, the Baishnabs are a special sect of Hinduism and their numbers are made up of converts from a variety of castes. They differ from the original Hindus in that they bury their dead and erect tombs. Many of the Baishnabs in the village are in comparatively favorable economic circumstances. Among them is one man who is a priest and who is supported by the income from a piece of land donated by a Zamindar of Raipur. The rest of the sect is engaged primarily in agriculture. The two Baishnab brothers who are the headmaster of the primary school and the village postmaster are counted among the influential persons of the village.

It is said that the Muslims settled in the village eight generations ago, and if we regard the body of Muslims as constituting a caste, they are the most numerous group apart from the Santals. Although there are no castes among the Muslims, we may discern caste-like stratifications among them. In Supur the upper stratum of the Muslims is composed of the Mirsahib, the Kajsahib, and the four Maulla families. By far the greater part of the rest of the Muslims are Seikhs whose social position is at the bottom of the lower stratum. There are a few opulent peasants among the Muslims, but most of them are tenant cultivators or agricultural laborers.

Caste and the Village Community

In the surveyed village of Supur the number of households in each caste is small with the exception of the Santals, Muslims, and Bag-dis. It is, therefore, not surprising to find that the various castes live intermingled in the village.

The group with the largest number of households, the Santals, live primarily in groups of houses at Nutumpukur in the Supur sector of the village, at Shetopukur in the Ramchandrapur sector, at Benipukur and Kulupukur in the Rasulganj sector, and at Chaurokdanga and Sabirganj in the Nurpur sector. All of these places are located on the periphery of the main inhabited area of the village. There are also a few groups of two or three households of Santals in the Nurpur sector, and in every case these groups of houses are located on lines joining the larger Santal agglomerations. The Santals' way of life differs from that of the rest of the village, and their relation to the village as a whole is reflected in the geographical distribution of their houses. There are no members of other castes living among them.

The Muslims live in two groups, the first consisting of thirty households arranged in three small agglomerations in an area near the primary school and southeast of the main inhabited area of the village. The other consists of fourteen households at Sabirganj and adjoins the agglomeration of the Santals.

In these cases also we may infer that the distribution of the houses put some distance between the life of the community and that of the Hindu villagers in the main inhabited area.

Among the Hindu villagers, the members of the Dhopa caste live together in a single residential area. In this region the residential subdivisions of a village are called *paras*, and the Dhopas live in the Dhopa *para* along one of the principal roads of the village. This residential area is adjoined by the Baidya *para*, a residential area which contains only a few households but whose name recalls the fact that it was once inhabited by members of the higher castes.

Other members of the upper and middle strata castes live in parts of the village in which the castes are intermingled, the exceptions being the Baishnabs who live in the Baishnab *para* in the Ramchandrapur sector and the Tambulis who live at Hat Tara in the Rasulganj sector. The area in which the castes are intermingled is the only one in which members of the lower castes live alongside members of the higher castes. For example, in Ralbazar (also called the Tambuli *para*), the main street of the village, we find not only members of the Tambuli, Napit, and Modok castes, but also Suris and Goalas. Again, in the Shakari *para*, where the president of the *panchayat* lives, we find not only members of such castes as the Sado-gopes and the Vaisya Sahas, but also the Kolus or Gorains, a lower caste.

In spite of this, in no case do the untouchables live in the same residential area as members of the castes in the upper and middle strata. The Bagdis, a relatively populous caste, are concentrated in two agglomerations in the western part of the Supur sector and the southern part of the Ramchandrapur sector. Members of the lowest castes, the Bauris, Muchis, Haris, and Koras—each live in a *para* bearing the name of their caste on the periphery of the main inhabited area; the lowest castes with fewer households build their huts in the vicinity of these residential areas. Among the refugees from East Bengal, by far the greater part of the Nama Sudra caste do live in the mixed residential area of the village but are distributed throughout parts of the village inhabited by members of the lowest castes.

The distribution of housing in the village thus clearly hints at the existence of a line of social demarcation separating the untouchables and tribal peoples from the rest of the population.

In this region, as elsewhere, the Brahmins hold the ritually highest position in the caste hierarchy, and the Baidyas are subordinate to them. The "nine castes" are considered to be of equal status, and they are allowed to inter-dine. A high-caste Baidya may even receive water from a member of one of the nine castes. It is expected that members of the lower castes, being included in the scheduled castes, will be treated differently from the members of the middle stratum nine castes.

As is suggested by the mixed character of some of the residential areas, the villagers do not discriminate against the lower castes in the course of everyday life as they do against the untouchables. It appears that members of the lower castes can drink tea with members of the higher castes without the least restraint, and we received the impression that there is almost no difference between those members of the lower castes whose economic position is good and members of the middle stratum. Some members of the castes in the upper and middle strata boast that the decline of caste discrimination is a sign of the progressive character of the Bengalis. Most

of the village ponds in the region are owned by individuals, but anyone is allowed to draw water from them, to bathe in them, or to
wash clothes in them. The only form of discrimination in this matter
arises from the fact that the people of the lowest castes use the ponds
near their homes, so that a distinction naturally arises between the
ponds used by the lowest castes and those used by the members of
other castes. A similar situation occurs in the use of wells. Until
thirty years ago there were only two wells, one belonging to the
Zamindar and the other to one of the Baidyas. Since that time six
public wells and three private wells have been dug. These wells,
and more particularly the public wells, can be used by anyone.
Each person uses his own rope and bucket to draw water, and no
restriction is imposed. In practice, however, the members of the
lowest castes live on the periphery of the village far from the wells
and hardly ever use them because they do not have the necessary
ropes and buckets; but we may say that, in principle, all caste distinctions in regard to the water supply have ceased to exist.

Differences among the various strata of the village community
are clearly apparent in the ceremonies performed for marriages or
funerals. The officiating priests who serve the upper and middle
castes are Brahmins who come from the neighboring village of
Rajatpur. Different Brahmins serve the higher castes and the "nine
castes," but this does not mean that there is a status difference
among the Brahmins. The lower castes all look to the poorer Brahmins who live outside the village for the performance of religious
services. There is a clear social distinction between these poor Brahmins and the Brahmins who perform religious services for the members of the upper and middle castes.

Social discrimination on the basis of caste is preserved in its original form among the lowest stratum of the village community. These
people cannot avail themselves of the services of the Napit, and they
must have their hair cut by a barber who is one of them or go some
distance into Bolpur. It is quite clear that members of these castes
are conscious of the status-rankings of the castes and that the cobbler
of the Muchi caste looks down on the snake-skin curer of the Bedia
Mal caste.

On the whole, however, caste discrimination is declining, and it
is not so much in evidence as in Samiala. The horizontal association
groups in the castes are not of sufficient strength to merit descrip-

tion. The caste *panchayats* range over wide geographical areas, depending on the numbers of the caste in question, and may comprise between five and fifteen villages. In principle, every caste has a caste *panchayat* with several officials and a headman. It is difficult to generalize about the function of these *panchayats*; they do not have a clearly defined character.

The members of the village castes are all conscious of belonging to their particular caste, but there is little sign of conflicts arising between them as a result of this consciousness. This does not mean, of course, that caste is no longer of any significance in the village community. Untouchability still remains, and the status-rankings of the upper, middle, and lower strata of the village community have not disappeared.

As we have already noted, most of the traditional caste occupations have been abandoned in the surveyed village and the *jajmani* system, a former source of social cohesion within the caste, has now completely disintegrated. The only survival of this institution is to be found in the yearly gifts of food-grain to the blacksmith from his middle and lower strata peasant clientele and to the Napits by some of the richer inhabitants of the village. Most purchases are made in Bolpur market, and within the village itself the cloth woven by the Sadogope caste, the sweetmeats made by the Modok caste, and the shell ornaments made by the Shakari caste are all bought for cash. The great majority of the inhabitants are peasants or agricultural laborers; villagers belonging to different castes are brought into relation with one another as a result of the employment of agricultural laborers by landowners, but this relation is not of such a nature that it could become a fixed relation of dependence of the type which characterizes feudal society.

The structure of power within the village community is thus dependent, in the last analysis, on the economic resources of the inhabitants. However, the castes whose members have economic resources at their command comprise only a few households, and we cannot pick out any one dominant caste similar to the Patidar caste in the Gujarat village. This does not mean, of course, that in the past there was no caste in the village which could be described as the dominant caste. In the days when the village was a flourishing market the Tambulis were strong enough to stand up to the Baidyas.[13] Three generations ago, one of the Majumdar family in the Baidya caste grew up as the Zamindar, and after the decline of the Tambulis the Baidya caste, led by the Majumdar family, gained complete mastery of the village. In those glorious days the residence of the Majumdar family reared its imposing bulk in the center of the village like the castle of some feudal lord, and we may suppose that the building served as a symbol of the family's overwhelming power. At the same time, the temple which stands immediately to the west of the Zamindar office was not only the Majumdar's own temple but also functioned as a temple for the whole village. The *durga puja*, a religious rite which is celebrated with the utmost magnificence in this region, is performed at this temple for the benefit of all the people of the village, and the expense incurred is met by the subscriptions and rents from land donated by the Majumdar family. In these ways the influence of the Majumdar family, which has now left the village, is still present to the inhabitants of Supur. The Baidyas who live in the village still have considerable wealth, but they are no longer the ruling caste in the village. There are two or three families among the Tambulis who own large areas of land, but the Tambulis as a caste cannot be said to enjoy the position of a powerful caste. In any case, both of these castes now have too few households for them to function as a ruling class.

Consequently, the present dominant group in the village consists not of any specific caste or castes, but of those families which own much land and have considerable economic resources at their disposal. Further, we must admit that these people have ability, and we are not excluding persons who are in the lower stratum as far as caste membership is concerned. Apart from the Majumdars, the greatest landowner and a powerful person in the village is the Suri who runs the small village brewery. There is a Goala who is active as one of the managers of village politics. Another such is a man of the Dhopa caste who is endowed with some wealth and ability. It need hardly be said that recruitment into the dominant group does not extend down to the untouchables of the scheduled castes. There are about two households among the Muslims which own large areas of land, but the Muslims live at some distance from the main

[13] The Tambulis still keep up the *durga puja* among themselves, which reminds them of the days when they were strong enough to stand up to the Zamindar.

inhabited area of the village and are not included in the dominant group. This is one point in which Supur differs from Samiala.

III. Village Self-Government

The Rule of the Village by the Zamindars
    Since Bengal was one of the bases of British colonialism, village self-government in the region has been influenced to a greater degree than in other regions by the reforms which took place during the British colonial administration. The most important of these was the Permanent Zamindari Settlement of 1797. Until that time the village had been presided over by a hereditary headman called the *mandal*, and the land tax was paid by the village as an independent political unit managing its own affairs. After the Settlement the village was placed under the control of the Zamindars who collected taxes on behalf of the government, and the village suffered greatly from their extortion. It will be appropriate to look back at the state of village self-government before India gained her independence, and before the Zamindari system was abolished in 1955.
    Until 1955, the taxes levied from the Supur area as a whole were collected by three Zamindars: Mukharjee, the king of Uttrapara, a place near Calcutta; Singha, the Lord of Raipur, a village near by, and the Majumdar family who lived in Supur. The proportions of the land subject to these three Zamindars were different in the four Supur *moujas*, but over the village as a whole 60 per cent of the land was taxed by Singha, 25 per cent by Majumdar, and 15 per cent by Mukharjee.
    Mukharjee and Singha were Zamindars on a great scale, and Majumdar was no small Zamindar either. He collected taxes in the administrative areas of Supur and Bolpur as the *patnidar* of Lord Singha as well as acting as Zamindar in an area made up from four police-station units covering four or five villages. It is also said that he himself owned agricultural land amounting to 270 hectares. In general, the Zamindar had to pay in taxes to the Government a fixed sum amounting to no more than about 50 per cent of the taxes actually collected by him. He also received income from his rights over orchards, ponds, rivers, forests, etc. and a large part of the land directly owned by him was exempt from taxation. The Zamindar could thus receive an enormous income.

The Majumdar family employed the services of one *naib* or manager and two *gomosta*s or tax-collectors, together with a number of
clerks and two private policemen. Two persons of low status from
Bihar were enrolled as police, but the other personnel were of the
Brahmin or Baidya castes. In addition, the family also employed
about ten people as domestic servants from the middle castes and
agricultural laborers from the lowest castes. The family used
tenants on some of its agricultural holdings and managed itself some
of the land it owned. The person employed as *naib* was a Brahmin
from outside the village, and one of the *gomosta*s was the present
president of the *panchayat*. His father was *gomosta* to Mukharjee,
and he himself served for sixteen years as a *gomosta* of the Majumdar
family. The post of *mandal* was also hereditary in his family, but
under the Zamindari system the *mandal* did not have the powers of a
headman. Rather, the *mandal* had the duty of assisting the Zamindar
in tax-collection and land-surveying, and by virtue of his office he
was required to mediate in disputes among the villagers, to preserve
the peace, and to uphold justice in the village. However, it appears
that when the Zamindar himself lived in the village his own direct
control was more effective than that exercised by the *mandal*. There
were also between ten and fifteen *jotdars*, or direct tax payers, in
the village, including the *gomosta*. There was thus no one among the
village landowners (whose land-holdings were at the most 7 hectares and on the average about 3 hectares) who could stand up to
the power of the Zamindars. The influential members of the village
community could act only as political managers dependent on the
power and authority of the Majumdar family.

Under British rule the system of local government in this region
was called the Union Board System, and the unit of local self-
government was an area made up of about ten villages. The system
was replaced in 1959 by the *panchayat* system, but there are places
in Birbhum District (to which the surveyed village belongs) in
which the old institutions of local government still survive. The
Bolpur Block was one of those in which the change to the new system
of local government took place at a relatively early date.

The Union Board System was instituted from above by the British
colonial government, and there is no expression in the Bengali
language by which it may be denoted. Supur came under a Union
Board covering thirteen *mouja*s located on the northern bank of the

Ojoy river. The Board consisted of nine members elected from the area; they served for terms of four years, and elections to the Board took place in Supur. Four persons who were elected to the Board are still living—one Brahmin who is a coal merchant in Bolpur but who also owns land in the village, the present president of the *panchayat* (also a Brahmin), a money-lender of the Tambuli caste who is the present vice-president of the *panchayat*, and the largest landowner among the Muslims. The Brahmin coal merchant was the chairman of the Board before its abolition. Although Board members were chosen by vote, it appears that it was always the politically adept among the richer inhabitants of the village who were elected.

The office of the Board was first established at Rajatpur, a village adjacent to Supur in which a large number of Brahmins live, but before it was abolished the Board had moved its office to Supur because one of the Board members presented to the Board the office of the Zamindar Mukharjee which he had bought. A paid Brahmin clerk from Rajatpur was in charge of the office-work connected with the business of the Board, and policemen bearing the titles of *dafadar* and *chaukidar* reported to the office in rotation to receive orders. *Dafadar* is the title of the head of a body of *chaukidars*, and this Union Board had an establishment of one *dafadar* and six *chaukidars*. The clerks employed by the Board were Brahmins or members of the other upper castes but the policemen were drawn from the lowest Hari, Dome, Mete, and Bagdi castes.

The finances of the Union Board were supplied by local taxation levied in accordance with certain legal provisions and by grants from higher organs of government. But, because the grants were very small and the income from local taxation was inadequate, the Board was unable to undertake anything in the nature of public works in the villages. A natural result of this situation was that the chief demand made on the villagers was for unpaid corvée labor.

This point will be made clear by inspection of the budget and accounts of the Union Board in the years preceding its abolition, as shown in Table 15.

The collection of taxes was entrusted to a contractor who received a 10 per cent fee. The total income of the Board, including the income from the animal pound[14] and government grants, was about Rs 3,000, and half of it was required for the salaries of the

14 Domestic animals are put in the pound. This matter will be explained later.

TABLE 15. Budget and Accounts of the Union Board

	Income				Expenditure		
	1956	1957	1958		1956	1957	1958
Taxes	849.00	849.00	849.00	Police Salaries	864.00	864.00	864.00
Cost of Tax-Collection (10%)	84.00	84.00	84.00	Police Uniforms	52.60	52.60	51.40
Government Grant for Police Uniforms	435.00	435.00	435.00	Clerk's Salary	240.00	240.00	240.00
				Fuel for Police and Others	12.00	12.00	12.00
				Furniture, etc. for Office	115.40	115.40	116.60
				Expenditure in Tax-Collection	84.00	84.00	84.00
Total	1,368.00	1,368.00	1,368.00	Total	1,368.00	1,368.00	1,368.00
Union Rate	432.14	—	—	Expenditure in Tax-Collection	77.00	70.00	60.00
Taxes	766.75	700.00	600.00	Road Repairs	600.00	400.00	300.00
Cost of Tax-Collection (10%)	77.00	70.00	60.00	Repairs to Drains	150.00	75.00	125.00
Income from Pound	328.00	250.00	250.00	Irrigation Works	300.00	125.00	75.00
Grant in Aid	40.00	40.00	40.00	Refuse Disposal	10.00	10.00	10.00
				School	10.00	—	—
				Hospital	300.00	300.00	300.00
				Miscellaneous	196.88	80.00	80.00
Total	1,643.88	1,060.00	950.00	Total	1,643.88	1,060.00	950.00
Grand Total	3,011.88	2,428.00	2,318.00	Grand Total	3,011.88	2,428.00	2,318.00

* The figures for 1956 are those of the closed accounts of that year, those for 1957 are those of the accepted budget for that year, and those for 1958 are those of the proposed budget for that year.

clerk, *dafadar*, and *chaukidars.* Only a trifling sum was left for alloca-
tion to works undertaken by the Board, and what could be done
when such a sum must be spread over thirteen villages?
Thus, throughout the course of its long history, the Union Board
System always remained a formal system of village government imposed from above. Since there was little expectation of getting funds
from the Union Board, many of the public works undertaken in
Supur were financed by contributions from the Majumdar family
which meant that no change came about in the rule of the village
by the Zamindars as a result of the institution of the Union Board
System. It is true that the rich peasants of the higher castes who became members of the Board were able, by means of this institution,
to enter the ranks of the dominant group of the village, but there
was never any question of this leading to a weakening of the Majumdars' controlling power. Whether as members or as chairmen of the
Board they never had any alternative but to act within the framework of the rule of the Zamindars.

The Village Panchayat System
   When West Bengal embarked upon a program to abolish the
Zamindari system in 1955, the old order of Zamindar rule also began to dissolve. Another measure which had a similar effect was the
Estate Acquisition Act which passed the West Bengal legislature in
1953 and came into effect in 1957. This act imposed a limit on land-
holdings and ordered the redistribution of all land held in excess of
this limit.
   As a result of these changes, the Government began to collect
taxes directly. It was, of course, no simple matter to bring a completely new fiscal system into being all at once, nor was it easy to
replace the old land registers. For this reason tax officials are still
using copies of the old land registers dating from the period of
Zamindar rule and are employing as *tahasildars* (the lowest officers
of the tax-collection system) the *gomostas* formerly employed by the
Zamindars. In the surveyed village a Brahmin of Rajatpur village
who had been a *gomosta* to Lord Singha and had collected taxes in
six *moujas* (including Nurpur and Rasulganj) has been working as a
tahasildar since 1957 and deals with an additional six *moujas* (including Supur and Ramchandrapur).[15] The *tahasildars* work under the
   [15] The fixed salary which he receives from the state is only Rs 27 per month,.

direction of an Inspector who comes under the Junior Land Reform Officer of the Estate Acquisition Office of Bolpur Block. The collected tax money is sent directly to Birbhum District Office.

By these measures the Zamindars have been separated from the local fiscal organization and have lost an immensely rich source of income. The Zamindars of Supur have long since moved to Bolpur and have almost completely lost their pre-eminent position in the village. The present head of the family declares that he now has only 10.1 hectares of agricultural land and 3.3 hectares of house-lots, wasteland, and ponds in the village. The family residence has been abandoned and allowed to fall into ruin, and their former office building is occupied only by a Bagdi laborer kept there as a watchman. Apart from occasional visits by the youngest Majumdar brother, who lives in Bolpur, the family now has no connection with the village.

It was after changes such as these had taken place in the village that the new system of local self-government, the *panchayat* system, came into force in West Bengal State in 1957.

A Block Development Office (referred to by the villagers as "the BDO") was set up under the District Office, and the *panchayat* system was instituted under its direction and supervision. In the surveyed village the *panchayat*s came into being in July 1959, after elections had been held. At the same time as these village *panchayats* (or *gram panchayats*) were set up, a superior organization called the *anchol panchayat*, a re-organized form of the Union Board, was also instituted.

Two *gram panchayats* were created in the surveyed village, one for the three *moujas* of Supur, Ramchandrapur, and Rasulganj, and the other for Nurpur. This kind of schematism in creating areas of local government is fairly common in this region; it would seem that two *gram panchayats* were created in the village because Nurpur *mouja* had a large population, there being at that time a fairly large number of refugees living in a camp adjacent to Sabirganj in the Nurpur sector of the village.

and his main source of income is the commission which he receives on the taxes collected. The commission is calculated at the rate of 2.5% up to Rs 3,000, 3% up to Rs 5,000, 3.5% up to Rs 7,000, and 4% over Rs 7,000. He has a man of the Hari caste to do preparatory work for him in the villages. He is paid Rs 16 per month by the Government.

The first of these *panchayats*, the Supur *gram panchayat*, consists of nine members, four of whom are elected from Supur, two from Ramchandrapur, and three from Rasulganj. In Ramchandrapur and Rasulganj the number of candidates did not exceed the number of seats and so no voting took place, but in the Supur sector of the village there were seven candidates, the three unsuccessful candidates belonging to the Baidya, Bayen, and Bagdi castes. The electoral constituencies for the Nurpur *gram panchayat* were Nurpur (4 members), Sabirganj and Hetiadanga (3 members), and Hajrabaganj and Chaurkdanga (2 members). Voting took place except in the last-named constituencies; three of the four Muslim candidates, who had stood without much hope of being elected, were in fact unsuccessful.

The members of the two *panchayats* are indicated in Table 16. The table shows that the majority of the members of the Supur *panchayat* are farmers who own large areas of land and who belong to the upper economic levels of the village community. The president of the *panchayat* is called the *adhaksya*, and as we have mentioned already, he is a man of the Brahmin caste who was formerly a *gomosta* in the service of the Majumdar family. The vice-president is an influential member of the Tambuli caste who is also a money-lender. In comparison with the men in the Supur *panchayat*, the members of the Nurpur *panchayat* own a much smaller area of land, and we may infer that their political influence is correspondingly weaker. In the Nurpur sector of the village there are no great landowners apart from the Muslims, but the rich Muslim farmers who were members of the Union Board did not stand in the election, and the Muslim candidates who had relatively large land-holdings were unsuccessful.

The elected members of the *panchayats* in turn choose the members of the *anchol panchayat*, which covers a slightly larger area than that covered by the Union Board. There are 19 *mouja*s under this *panchayat*, which is called the Raipur-Supur *anchol panchayat*, and its members are drawn from eight *gram panchayat*s. The members chosen from the surveyed village include two members from the area of the Supur *panchayat* and one member from the area of the Nurpur *panchayat*. The members from Supur *panchayat* are one Brahmin who was the chairman of the old Union Board and one member of the Baishnab community who is the headmaster of a primary school in a neighboring village, while the member chosen by the Nurpur *panchayat* is of the Tambuli caste. The office of the *anchol panchayat* is located in the house of the president, who is called the *pradan*. He is a rich farmer and coal merchant of Raipur.

TABLE 16. Panchayat Members

Members of the Supur Panchayat

Name	Caste	Mouja	Occupation	Land-holding	Notes
P. Ray	Brahmin	Supur	Agriculture	13.5	President
P. Saha	Suri	Supur	Agriculture	9.9	Brewing
P. Dey	Tambuli	Rasulganj	Agriculture	6.8	Vice-President
K. Gosh	Goala	Supur	Agriculture	3.8	
H. Hazra	Dhopa	Supur	Agriculture	5.3	
H. Singha	Kayastha	Ramchandrapur	Agriculture	5.1	
M. Sarkar	Nama Sudra	Ramchandrapur	Agriculture	1.7	Refugee.
G. Badra	Tambuli	Rasulganj	Agriculture	3.3	Refugee
H. Nurm	Santal	Rasulganj	Agriculture	—	(tenant)

Members of the Nurpur Panchayat

Name	Caste	Mouja	Occupation	Land-holding	Notes
K. Pal	Tambuli	Nurpur	Businessman	—	President
S. Seick	Muslim	Sabirganj	Agriculture	0.6	
S. Dey	Tambuli	Nurpur	Agriculture	1.7	Bhidimaking
N. Modok	Modok	Nurpur	Agriculture	1.6	
K. Patra	Nama Sudra	Nurpur	Agriculture	1.1	Refugee
M. Mazi	Santal	Charokdanga	Agriculture	—	(tenant)
C. Mazi	Santal	Hajrabaganj	Agriculture	—	(tenant)
B. Mazi	Santal	Sabirganj	Agriculture	0.2	(tenant)
K. Mazi	Santal	Hetiadanga	Agriculture	—	(tenant)

The members of these *panchayats* serve three year terms. Elections were scheduled for 1962 but were postponed because of the state of emergency occasioned by the Sino-Indian border dispute. Local government is still being run by the *panchayats* which we have described.

The actual business of local government is, not surprisingly, meager since the surveyed village as a whole, with its 400 households, has barely Rs 2,500 at its disposal in each budgetary year. And this sum has recently been reduced by half. The greater part of the village income is derived from a grant out of local taxation collected by the *anchol panchayat*, but the Supur *panchayat* also has some income from the animal pound. The pound is a place in which animals which have strayed on agricultural land are kept until their owners pay a fine.[16] An auction is held among those who own buildings which could be used as the village pound, and the man who makes the highest bid is appointed pound-keeper. The pound is a source of income which the village *panchayat* can employ with some freedom, but in the last few years the income from the pound has decreased. A pound has also been set up in Rajatpur, and in 1962 the money paid at the auction of the pound dropped to Rs 260.

The funds available are thus very small, and quite inadequate when they are allotted among a number of items in accordance with a prearranged scheme. If the *panchayat* has Rs 50, it can use the money for some public work which will cost Rs 50; but in practice it has been found that larger sums are needed, and since the *panchayat* cannot levy additional contributions from the impoverished villagers, the work is usually done by means of unpaid corvée labor and by voluntary contributions from rich peasants who are to benefit from the work in question. This means that the *panchayat*s cannot undertake any work in an orderly and discreet manner.

The main income of the village *panchayat*s, however, comes to them under the arrangement by which the *anchol panchayat* levies an income tax and business and vehicle license taxes from the area under its jurisdiction and distributes part of the money to them. The *anchol panchayat* allocates funds out of the total made up from its income from taxation and the grants which it receives from the Government, after it has paid the salaries of its clerks, the salaries of the 2 *dafadars* and 15 *chaukidars* living in the various villages, and the expenses of administration and tax-collection (the commissions paid to the two tax-collectors). Table 18 shows the items of the *anchol panchayat* budget which relate to the administrative areas of Supur and Nurpur.

---

[16] These pounds are found all over India. There was no pound in the Gujarat village which we surveyed, but there were pounds in neighboring villages. The pound-keeper gives a reward to villagers who bring in stray cattle (Rs 0.5 in the case of oxen or water buffalo) and levies a fine from the owner (Rs 2.0 per ox and Rs. 2.5 per water buffalo for the first 24 hours). The pound-keeper retains any balance left after the *panchayat* have taken its quarterly fee.

TABLE 17.   Budgets and Accounts of the Village Panchayats

	Supur				Nurpur			
	1960–61	1961–62	First Half of 1961–62	1962–63	1960–61	1961–62	First Half of 1961–62	1962–63
Balance from Previous Year	160.89				45.75			
Government Grant	845.65	578.22	80.00	492.00	522.37	359.62	125.00	305.00
Subsidy			706.00					
Income from Pound	904.75	517.00	193.50	359.00			11.00	
Total Income	1,911.29	1,095.22	979.50	851.00	568.09	359.62	136.00	305.00
General Management								
a. Office	50.00	50.00	10.38	50.00	50.00	50.00	8.26	50.00
b. Contingency	50.00	50.00	52.00	50.00	50.00	50.00	37.50	
Rural Development								
a. Agriculture	50.00	50.00		50.00	50.00	30.00		30.00
b. Irrigation	50.00	100.00		50.00	50.00			10.00
c. Drinking Water	280.00	300.00	710.87	92.00	75.00	100.00		21.00
d. Roads	1,000.00	300.00	9.00	443.00	200.00	88.00	4.50	185.00
e. Miscellaneous	170.00							
Education								
a. Adult Education	100.00	36.00	36.00	36.00	20.00			
b. Primary School								
Miscellaneous	161.29	209.22		80.00	48.09	41.62	11.00	9.00
Total Expenditure	1,911.29	1,095.22	818.25	851.00	568.09	359.62	61.26	305.00

The figures for 1960–1961 are those of the closed accounts of that budgetary year.

As will be seen from the contents of the Table, the police are directly under the *anchol panchayat,* an arrangement which has been continued from the time of the Union Board.

However, the administration of the other items in the table has been handed over to the village *panchayats,* so that there is thus some degree of decentralization of authority. The budget of the village

TABLE 18.　Budget of the Anchol Panchayat, 1961–62

	Supur	*Nurpur*	*Total of Village Panchayats*
Government Grants			
a.　Chaukidars	180.00	90.00	1,170.00
b.　Dafadars	27.00	27.00	216.00
c.　Clerks	120.00	120.00	966.00
Lump Taxes for Police Grant	125.00	125.00	1,000.00
a.　Income Tax	520.45	314.45	3,723.71
b.　Business Licenses	5.00	6.00	72.00
c.　Vehicle Licenses	93.00	67.50	963.00
Block Development Office Grant	10.00	10.00	80.00
Land Income*	136.00	21.50	961.28
Balance from Previous Year	64.96	64.00	515.96
Total Income	1,281.91	845.45	9,692.00
Chaukidars'　Salaries	360.00	180.00	2,340.00
Equipment	13.72	6.86	89.18
Dafadars'　Salaries	54.00	54.00	432.00
Equipment	2.47	2.47	16.94
Clerks' Salaries	120.00	120.00	960.00
Travelling Allowances	13.00	13.00	100.00
Contingencies	44.00	44.00	350.00
Miscellaneous	12.50	12.50	100.00
Commission on Tax-Collection	65.00	40.00	500.00
Number Plates for Carts	5.00	10.00	150.00
Oil for Dafadars	4.00	3.50	29.22
Total Expenditure	703.69	485.83	5,243.45
Allotment to Village Panchayat	578.22	359.62	4,428.55

* In former times *chaukidars* were given land in some villages. These figures represent the income from such land.

panchayat must receive the approval of the *gram saba* or general meeting of the village. In comparison with the form of local government carried on at the time of the Union Board, when nine committee members made all decisions for a larger administrative area, local government has been democratized. However, funds are available on so small a scale that the newly-created village *pancha-yats* are only able to carry on activities of a negative character.

As we have said, the combined offices of the Supur and Nurpur village *panchayats* are located in the building formerly used as a tax-collection office by the Zamindar, Mukharjee. There is much less documentary material in this office than in the village office in Samiala. Although the two *panchayats* were organized separately, they hold their meetings at the same time in the office building, and the *adhaksya* of the Supur *panchayat* records the proceedings of both meetings. As a matter of form, this *adhaksya*, a Brahmin, becomes the secretary of the Nurpur village *panchayat* when the business of the Nurpur *panchayat* is being conducted, and the *adhaksya* of the Nurpur village *panchayat* only signs the minutes. The Brahmin performs the functions of the heads of both *panchayats* and is thus the virtual headman of the whole village. Announcements of *panchayat* meetings are communicated to the members by a *chaukidar*. The meetings are held once a month, but the minutes show that they are often adjourned for lack of a quorum. Discussion at these meetings centers on the question of how best to use the small grants made by the Government. It is difficult to make progress in such business, and whenever the *panchayats* undertake public works—usually, road repairs, the digging of wells, and the building of irrigation channels—they must hold many meetings and repeatedly revise the plans which they submit for a government grant. It is quite clear that the village itself could never contemplate undertaking public works on its own account.

Problems Connected with Village Self-Government

The problem which we must consider in connection with the *panchayat* system in the surveyed village is the fact that two *pan-chayats* have been set up in mechanical conformity to an administrative scheme although the area concerned constitutes a single village. That neither the members of the *panchayats* nor the majority of the village inhabitants think there is anything objectionable in this mechanical division into two *panchayats* is no doubt due to the fact that they feel no inconvenience under the present weak *panchayat* system; it also shows that the *panchayats* were instituted from above, that the villagers are acting in blind obedience to the powers that be, and that great power is wielded by government officials.

For example, the duties of the *panchayat* are stipulated by government officials, the minutes of the *panchayat* meetings must be inspected four times a year by an inspector from the Block Development Office. Again, *panchayat* accounts are inspected by an auditor from the Sub-Division Office, an office intermediate between the BDO and the District Office. Nearly all the public works undertaken by the *panchayats* are dependent on funds which are passed down through these various offices. This means that there is very little scope for real self-government on the part of the village, and in the background lies the fundamental reason for the existence of this situation—the poverty of the villagers which makes it almost impossible to raise any funds once the land-tax has been paid. In this region, where the villages have no financial resources of their own, the *panchayat* system is liable to be of a purely formal nature, and under the present circumstances the situation is inevitable.

This, however, does not alter the fact that the *panchayat* is the political and administrative organ of government in the village. To say that the *panchayat* system has been artificially contrived by the government bureaucracy does not imply that real village self-government is being carried on within the framework of some other traditional form of political organization. In this region the traditional form of village self-government was overthrown by the rule of the Zamindars, and the *panchayat*, although it may not be able to fulfill a positive function, is still the organ of village self-government both in name and in fact.

It is for these reasons that, in general, the membership of the *panchayats* is made up of those persons in the village community who are the actual possessors of political influence. The members representing the untouchables and tribal peoples are only nominal members, and they seldom attend the meetings of the *panchayats*. If we exclude them, we may say that the members of the *panchayats* are the influential inhabitants of the village and the real holders of power within the village community, but they are not outstanding men of proved ability. The Brahmin *adhaksya* is the virtual headman of the whole village of Supur, but he is not strong enough to hold down the rich farmers and Tambuli money-lender who is his vice-president. In spite of this, conflict among factions in the *panchayat* is almost unknown because the *panchayat* are unable to undertake any work which might give rise to serious conflicts of material interest. The castes are too small for inter-caste conflicts to manifest themselves in village self-government, nor do the castes display much cohesion as social groups. The members of the dominant group thus co-operate in running the *panchayats* in a manner which transcends caste.

The *panchayats* in this village are, therefore, not controlled by members of a dominant caste, but are controlled by a body of landowners whose membership extends down to the lower castes. Nor is this all, for of the *panchayat* members only the *adhaksya* and a Kayastha refugee are upper caste—so the main body of the actual influential group in the village is made up of rich farmers from the middle and lower strata of the village community. This, of course, does not mean that the power of the upper castes has disintegrated. The prestige which the Baidya caste enjoyed in the time of the Zamindars still survives. We cannot overlook the influence exerted by the Zamindar families who still make donations to village funds on all manner of occasions, nor can we overlook the influence of an old man of the Baidya caste who has returned to the village on his retirement from the post of headmaster of a high school. Even the *adhaksya* must bow his head before the ex-headmaster when it comes to interpreting official documents written in bureaucratic English. In spite of these things, however, one can scarcely deny that the dominant group in village government is divorced from caste affiliations and that it is the possession of wealth which its members have in common. This means that the character of the village is different in certain respects from that of the Gujarat village which we have analysed—a difference which is indicated by the fact that the activities of the Supur *panchayats* are even more feeble than in the case of the Gujarat village and which is due to differences in the organization of the two villages.

IV. CHANGES IN VILLAGE ORGANIZATION

Past Changes and the Present Condition of the Village Community
    As we have already said, the Supur village community has undergone great changes since the railway station was built at Bolpur. The high-caste Baidyas and the rich Tambulis have left the village.

At the same time, caste discrimination in the course of everyday life has almost disappeared among the various strata. During the period in which the Zamindars held overwhelming power, perhaps a certain degree of levelling took place among the other inhabitants of the village, and those who succeeded in holding on to their land in a period of social change, as well as those who had gained possession of land and had risen in the world, regarded themselves as "the others" in a world which consisted of "Zamindars and the others." The people of the lowest castes were, of course, not included in this consciousness of belonging to "the others," and they were in fact separated by a strict line of demarcation.

There is reason to believe that when the Zamindari system was abolished after Indian independence, the effect produced was that of accentuating the levelling tendency in the community since the passing of the Zamindars left the village without any outstanding figures at the upper end of the social scale. The Zamindars were not only the possessors of rights as tax-collectors but were also great landowners, and the land owned by the Majumdar family was not confined to its holdings in Supur. They still own land within the prescribed legal limits in Supur and Bolpur. The re-distribution of land under the land reform has not resulted in the mass transformation of the peasantry into cultivating proprietors. Consequently, there have been no great changes in social stratification in the village, and the existing stratification has remained intact. That is to say, the village still retains its polarized structure consisting on the one hand of rich farmers who employ agricultural laborers and on the other of landless agricultural laborers and temporary workers. It is probably unnecessary to point out once more that the former are drawn from all the upper, middle, and lower castes in the village community while the latter are members of the group of lowest castes.

It is true that the abolition of the Zamindari system and the introduction of the panchayats system have brought about changes in the structure of village political power. The removal of the power concentrated in the hands of the Zamindars has given greater scope to those who take part in the operation of local self-government. When the Zamindars were in power, their gomostas and the influential members of the upper and middle castes constituted a dominant group which functioned by virtue of the power of the Zamindars.

But now persons from the lower castes who have some economic resources are included among the active members of the *panchayats*. These developments have accentuated the levelling tendency among the castes in the upper, middle, and lower strata of the village community but have done nothing to narrow the gap which separates them from the untouchables and tribal peoples.

The rich farmers who do not need to work are supported in idleness by cheap surplus labor. They have not the slightest desire to improve agricultural technology or production and are content if their control of the village community is secure. Among them are some who not only do not aspire to take part in the democratic developments which have taken place in the village, but are so addicted to idleness and parasitism that they have taken to drink. Responsible villagers decry the village bosses' lack of interest in public questions, and their criticism is legitimate. That they do not take to crime is probably only due to the fact that the organs of village government are not granted sufficient funds to make peculation worth their while. The members of the lowest stratum must work to the limit of their strength if they are to make a living, and they are conscious of being discriminated against as untouchables, but they have not even been granted the wherewithal to resist such discrimination.

Change and Stagnation in the Village Community

The people of the lowest stratum are thus still the exploited group in the village community, and they have been excluded from the patterns of life of the other inhabitants of the village. They participate in village activities only as the employees of the villagers or as *chaukidars*, that is, as policemen and messengers. It was an unprecedented change, in form at least, for them to have representatives in the *panchayats*, but they do not show any inclination to take part in the deliberations of these bodies. They are buried in ignorance and poverty.

In order to help these people, the Department of Rural Development of Visva-Bharati University has started an adult education extension program in the village. Two of the villagers (the postmaster and the headmaster of the primary school) have been employed as teachers of social studies and "literacy;" semester courses are given for the untouchables and Santals every evening except during the busier agricultural seasons. However, it is usual for only twenty members of a class of forty (with ages ranging from 10 to 40) to appear in the classroom, and even those who do attend do not learn very much. They do not feel any necessity to learn, and for the same reason, they hardly ever send their children to the primary school.

There is no sign that the ignorance and poverty of the lowest stratum is being overcome and, likewise, there have been no spectacular changes among the classes above them. The Block Development Office sends extension workers to the villages in an attempt to improve agricultural production, but so large is the area covered that the extension workers are unable to visit the villages very frequently. The rich farmers of the upper stratum, as we have noted, have no desire to adopt new forms of technology. The state administration has been instituting agricultural co-operatives, and an agricultural co-operative was organized in the village in 1962, but it has only a nominal existence.

It is therefore difficult to entertain any hope that the village will undergo any marked changes in the near future. Those influential villagers who boast that the absence of caste discrimination in West Bengal shows the progressive character of the Bengalis do not appear to feel any inclination to carry their egalitarianism one step further and treat the members of the lowest stratum as fellow villagers. Nor can we discover in them any inclination to make alterations in agricultural technology which will lead to progressive developments in the village community. Unless something unforeseen occurs, we must expect the stagnation of the village to continue.

There is, however, one point which deserves our attention. It is impossible to predict how many of the refugees from East Bengal will be accepted into the upper stratum of the village community or, further, how many of them will be able to rise higher in the village social scale than the long-established influential families. Yet it is certain that in the process of trying to advance themselves socially, the able people among these newly arrived refugees will raise new problems in the village, and they may be the means of bringing to an end the present stagnant condition of the village community.

It is improbable that such developments will occur on a scale sufficient to bring about changes throughout the whole village community, nor will the developments be of such a character as to do this. As we have said in connection with the Gujarat village, not until untouchability has been overcome can it be said that a radical alteration has taken place in the Hindu village community. To do this is extremely difficult, even in Supur, and improvements in the economic condition of a minority group of refugees do not entail the prospect of overcoming untouchability.

3. TWO TYPES OF JAPANESE
VILLAGE STRUCTURE

In my *Nihon Nōson no Shakaiteki Seikaku* (The Social Character of the Japanese Village),[1] I classified Japanese villages as villages of *dōzoku* (clan) or *kōgumi* (club) structure. Originally, the word *dōzoku* denoted a patrilineal kinship group and *kōgumi* a grouping of people to worship Shinto or Buddhist images. The clan-type villages consist of powerful stem families and consanguineous branch families bound together by a parent-child, or master-servant, relationship. Such a status relationship is absent in the club-type villages: the villagers have associated together to form a village; they are equal in status and take turns acting as the leader. In the book mentioned above, I argued that the clan-type village developed into a communal village which retained some features of the clan.

The following are survey reports of two villages, one in Akita prefecture and the other in Okayama. The surveys were conducted during the postwar land reform, and the reports were originally published in the book cited above. Needless to say, since the land reform all but destroyed the landlord system which is the basis of the *dōzoku* system, it is extremely difficult to find a typical clan village in contemporary rural society.

A) A Clan-Type Village in an Underdeveloped Area

I. A SKETCH OF THE VILLAGE

Tatehana is located in the administrative village[2] of Shimokawa-zoi in Akita prefecture. Until the end of the Tokugawa period this

[1] The University of Tokyo Press, 1949.

[2] The term "administrative village" refers to territorial units established by the national government in 1889. An administrative village contains a number of natural communities. As used here, the term "village" refers to a natural community.

community was part of Hitsuzaki village across the Yoneshiro River. According to the 1872 registration, the village consisted of 30 families: 13 surnamed Nagasaki; 9, Nakajima; 6, Kamada; 1, Maruoka; and 1, Abukawa. Economically, the families were ranked as follows: 1 family was taxed annually on the basis of 27.6 *koku* of rice; 1 family, 12.4 *koku*; 5 families, 5–7 *koku*; 6 families, 3–5 *koku*; 12 families, 1–3 *koku*; and 5 families, less than 1 *koku*.[3] The family with the 27.6 *koku* annual assessment was the main family of the Nagasaki clan. The family settled in Tatehana after the Nakajima clan but with the economic backing of its stem-family, an extremely wealthy family in the original Nagasaki family in Hitsuzaki, seems to have overwhelmed the older Nakajima group.

The present number of families, including post-war repatriates, is fifty-six. When the railroad employee, the school teacher, and others who are not an integral part of the community are excluded, the number is reduced to fifty families. Forty-eight of these are farmers. Since the beginning of the Meiji period, three families have moved into the community. Seven branch families (*bunke*) were established during the Meiji period (1868–1912), six during the Taisho (1912–1926), and ten during the Showa (1926–present). Reclamation of 3.5 *chō* and 4.5 *chō* of land along the Yoneshiro River in 1913 and 1931 may have contributed to the population increase. The distribution of families in terms of present economic class is shown in Table 1.

TABLE 1.   Composition of Farming Households (1)

Land cultivated (in *chō*)	Land-* owner	Owner- farmer	Owner-* tenant	Tenant-* owner	Tenant	Total
0— .3	1	0	1	0	1	3
.3— .5	0	0	1	1	2	4
.5—1.0	0	3	0	4	4	11
1.0—1.5	0	1	3	3	4	11
1.5—2.0	1	3	5	4	3	16
2.0—3.0	0	0	1	1	0	2
3.0—4.0	0	0	0	1	0	1
Total	2	7	11	14	14	48

* Landowners cultivate some of their own land and rent out the remainder. An owner-tenant and a tenant-owner cultivate their own and rented land, but the former owns more land than he rents while the latter rents more land than he owns.

[3] The tax rate was about one-half a farmer's annual yield; one *koku* is approximately 5.2 bushels.

Comparable data for the early Meiji period indicates that there were 4 landowners, 4 owner-farmers, 10 owner-tenants, 9 tenant-owners, and 3 tenants living in the village. Since the Meiji period the number of tenants has increased appreciably. An analysis of the history of each family discloses considerable fluctuation in the family fortunes. The Nagasaki main family owns 11.6 *chō* of farm land and is easily the wealthiest family in the village. Its influence in the village has been drastically reduced, however, since it cut the area of family-cultivated land to 2 *chō* in 1920, 1 *chō* in the mid-1920's, and ceased to have any such land in 1941. The main family of the Nakajima clan, which in the early Meiji period had an annual assessed yield of only 3.2 *koku*, is the second wealthiest family in Tatehana. This family is followed by a Kamada main family, whose tax rank in the early Meiji period was something less than 12.4 *koku*. (The main family of the entire Kamada clan has ceased to

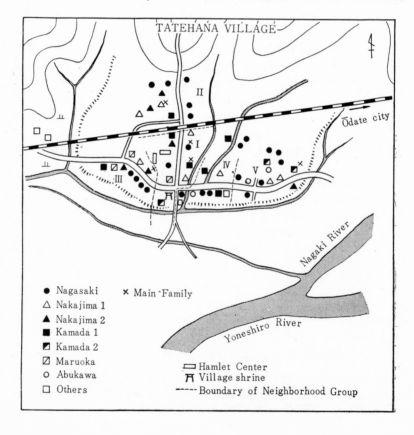

exist, and the clan has divided into two sub-clans.) Since the beginning of Meiji much Tatehana land has become the property of landlords in the nearby city of Ōdate.

Since depiction of the northeastern clan village would be inac-
curate if we relied on data from this village alone, we have added
survey data from Niida, a village near Ōdate. Niida has long been
controlled by two landlords, Ichinoseki and Adachi, who at the
height of their prosperity owned 120 *chō* and 80 *chō*. The Adachi
main family has declined, but the Ichinoseki family enjoys a high
status in the community. The present Ichinoseki main family is the
twelfth generation since the clan's settlement in Niida. It became
wealthy some six or seven generations ago when it began selling
liquor as a supplementary occupation. The data regarding this village are based on interviews with the Ichinoseki main and branch
families and with branches of the Adachi clan.

II. ANI AND OJI

The Japanese emphasis of primogeniture and patrilineal descent
is best exemplified in the almost universal distinction made between
the family's eldest (*ani*) and junior (*oji*) sons. In a word, the eldest
son succeeds to the family inheritance; the junior sons must, as the
saying goes, "be contented with cold rice."

In Tatehana and Niida, the eldest son is called *ani* and junior
sons *onji* (a cognate of *oji*). The eldest son is treated from childhood
as the family heir,[4] junior sons are regarded as a source of labor, a
status which they themselves accept as proper. A small landowner-
cultivator commented: "I would set up the third or the fourth
rather than the second son as a branch family. The second son is
so close in age to the first that it is hard for the older brother to control him. On the other hand, if the eldest continues to house the
second son, he will begin expecting his first child about the time
the family must begin looking for a wife for the second son. Then
he would soon have his children. You simply add more mouths to
feed, which is not economically desirable." If there are too many
sons in the family, or if the family cultivates such a small piece of

---

[4] Each family has its own tradition which is inculcated into its members. The
wealthier the family, the more strict the inculcation. It is the eldest son who is
most thoroughly educated in the family tradition.

land that the junior sons' labor is unnecessary, the younger sons are
expected to emigrate from the village. If the family is well-to-do,
the junior sons may be sent to high school and become teachers or
white collar workers; but if the family is poor, they may became
artisans or laborers. In the past, the more fortunate might marry an
eldest daughter and become the heir to her family's property. More
frequently, a junior son worked for a landlord and later become
his tenant. The range of opportunities open to younger sons has
expanded since the Meiji era, but new opportunities are still limited and have not radically improved the inferior status of junior
sons. Their emigration from their home village is forced, and the
world which receives them takes them in simply as inexpensive
labor.

What happens to a junior son who does not emigrate, but remains
in the village? He remains with his family and farms, hoping that
the family head will set him up as a branch house. When the junior
son reaches a marriageable age, he is espoused but is not immediately separated as a branch family. He continues to work for the
family[5] in a master-servant relationship which lasts for about ten
years.[6] His status during this period is, of course, better than a
servant's but it is far below that of the eldest son.[7] Put in extreme
terms, the eldest son and a junior son are born as different kinds of
human beings, as is evident in the terms used in wealthier families
by the eldest son's children and by co-resident junior sons' children.
The term for father in this area is *dodo* and for mother, *aba*.[8] The

[5] Because of the presence of collateral relatives, the family structure of this
area is complex and the family size large in comparison with Kawairi village
(see the next chapter). Incidentally, the marriage age of junior sons tends to be
later than that of the eldest son, who marries early to secure additional labor.

[6] There is a trend toward shortening the junior son's period of service to the
main family. In this area a junior son customarily works for the main family
until he is 41 years of age, but if he dies before his branch house is set up, his
son will branch out from the main family when he is 30 years old.

[7] This distinction is sharpest among the upper classes of the village. For example, in one family the eldest son is preoccupied with community affairs, and
the farm work is done by junior sons. In another family, the eldest son works at
the village office and his brother-in-law looks after the farm. In poorer families
such a distinction between eldest and junior sons cannot arise for economic
reasons.

[8] In the lower classes in this village, the term for father is *ide* and for mother,
appa. Grandfather and grandmother are called *jisama* and *basama* in the upper
classes and *jitcha* and *baba* in the lower classes. Kinship terminology is thus
determined by social class, but such class distinctions are few in this village.
Villages with many such distinctions are found in the nearby mountainous areas.

eldest son's children call a junior son and his wife *onji* and *umba*, or simply by their given names, while a junior son's children call the eldest son and his wife *dodo* and *aba*. Moreover, the eldest son's children call a junior son's children by their given names, even if they are older, and the latter call the former *ani* even if they are younger. Also, the oldest son's wife is called *ane*; a junior son's wife is called *umba*. The terms used for the eldest son and his family members and for a junior son and his family members connote superior and inferior statuses and indicate their master-servant relationship, over and above that of kinship.

After a period of co-residence a junior son establishes a branch family, called *bekke* in this area. The material basis of this branch house is given as a reward for the son's years of service to the main family. The grant either pays for the building of a new house or buys an old one and provides the necessities for farming, draft animals, and farm implements. Since the amount of land given to a branch family is extremely small, it is impossible to subsist on the land granted, except in the richest families, and the main family then provides land for the branch house to rent. If the main family does not have land to rent, the branch must rent land from the parent family of its main family. Since the main family must supplement what it gives with rented land, the master-servant relationship between the eldest and junior sons continues after branching.

III. THE MAIN FAMILY AND THE BRANCH FAMILY

The above discussion indicates that it is impossible for the branch family to become independent of the main family. Establishment of a branch is, besides being a reward to a junior son, a basis for the perpetuation of the main family. If the kinship relation between the main and branch or sub-branch families is supplemented by a tenancy relationship, it then has an economic basis as well.

Branches are expected to manifest their loyalty to the main family at the New Year and *o-bon* celebrations by the performance of certain rituals. On January 1 or 2, branch families visit the main family, present rice cakes, give their New Year's greetings, and in turn receive New Year's treats. At *o-bon*, after returning from the family graveyard, they go to the main house for ancestor veneration.

At marriages, funerals, and all family ritual gatherings, the main family takes charge of the ceremonies and its family head officiates. At the marriage of a family member, guests stay at the main family's home and, after the wedding, are invited by the main family to a banquet.[9] In Tatehana some religious groups (*ko*) were organized around a main family.

Main and branch families cooperate also in farming. For example, when the Nagasaki main family still farmed, almost all of its twenty sub-families gathered at the main house to decide the schedule for transplanting the rice seedlings. Later, the branches formed several cooperative groups and the main family sent its servant to help transplant the seedlings. Members of the Nakajima clan are also accustomed to gathering at the main house, determining the transplanting schedule over drinks, and then cooperating in the work.[10]

The main family must fulfill the obligations of master, or overlord, of the clan, but in the final analysis, its authority, depends on its economic resources. It must provide economic assistance to branch families when they are hard-pressed, counsel them when asked, lend them dinner ware and furniture when needed, and treat them at clan celebrations several times a year. A member of a branch family may visit the main family uninvited and expect to be entertained by it; he may also ask the main family for food if he does not have enough to eat; he does not hesitate helping the main family whenever it seems necessary, even if he is not asked to do so. The *dōzoku* is thus family writ large, with the main family as its head. The main family derives its authority as the patriarch of this extended family from its relationships of mutual dependence with the branch families. It is true that the greater the authority of the main family, the stronger is the feeling of the branches that the main family is the overlord and they are its vassals;[11] but such feeling does not dissipate the family atmosphere of the clan.

The main family considers a sub-branch a "grandchild" branch,

---

[9] If the main family is powerful, it can control marriages of clan members.

[10] The expenses for the meals on transplantation days are usually met by the main family, for whom the transplantation is done first. Since the Nagasaki main family was the coordinator of these activities while it maintained its farm, its cessation of farming was probably a serious blow to the solidarity of the clan.

[11] Even now there is the tradition that the landowner-main families are the only literate group; the feeling persists that the branches are to do any work that involves physical labor and that the main-family is to do mental work.

and the sub-branch considers the main family its grand-main family. Since the two families are related through a third family, a sub-branch is like a vassal of a vassal. The relationship between a sub-branch and its parent family repeats the relationship between the main family of the clan and its direct branches. If the main family is wealthy enough to rent land to its sub-branches, the solidarity of the clan is strengthened.[12]

Occasionally a segment of the clan does gain wealth and become independent. This may occur when the genealogical relation between the main house and one of its segments becomes distant, when the main family loses its economic base and the branches can no longer depend on it, or when a branch gains wealth rivaling the main family's and begins to have its own branches. In Tatehana, the Nagasaki clan remains a single unit, but six of the fifteen Nakajima families have formed their own *dōzoku*. Traditionally, the main-branch relationship extends down to the grandchild families as long as the main family has the economic resources to maintain the clan.

There are also non-consanguineal branches established by servants. This type of branch is called *yashinai-bekke* as contrasted with the consanguineal *miwakare-bekke*. The one such branch in Tatehana was established in the Nagasaki clan. The father of the present head of this non-consanguineal branch lived with and worked for the Nagasaki main family, from his youth, as a servant. He married at 23 and remained with the family until he died at the age of 40. His son—the present head—was then 14 years old. His wife continued to work for the main family for another year, when the main family gave them a house and rented them .2 *chō* of rice paddy and .05 *chō* of dry field, thereby setting them up as a branch. At present this branch rents .2 *chō* of land from its main family and .5 *chō* from another landlord. Such a pathetically small reward after some twenty years of service seems like extreme exploitation, but for the man concerned, it is *on*, a great favor done by the main family. The main family played an important part in the marriage of the pres-

---

[12] Since the branch family usually lacks resources, the main family commonly establishes a sub-branch. Often, a junior son of a branch family will work for the main family for a period of time and then branch out from the main family. In such case, however, the new branch is equal in status to its parent family and cannot be regarded its branch.

ent family head, and an intimate main-branch relationship has developed between them. The branch is not only a tenant of the main family, but goes to the main house to give New Year and *o-bon* greetings just like the consanguineal branches. Its status is somewhat lower than the direct branches but the differences between them are slight.

Large landholders commonly have non-consanguineal branches. For example, of the twenty-one branches in the Niida Ichinoseki clan, nine are non-consanguineal branches and six are their subbranches. These Ichinoseki non-consanguineal branches are usually provided with 1.5–2.0 *chō* of rented land and are all tenants of the clan's main family. Some of the non-consanguineal branches came to this village with the main family, and some were established as recently as thirty years ago. They have all been given the privilege of assuming the surname of the main family. Although its main family has declined in importance, the Adachi clan of Niida has non-consanguineal branches too. In general, in this area, there are more non-consanguineal than consanguineal branches in the *dōzoku* with the larger landlords.[13] In these groups the clear status differ-

---

[13] In the nearby village of Nittame during the Tokugawa period the head of the Saito clan owned 20 *chō* of land and was village headman. Only four of the clan's twenty-eight branches are consanguineal; the remainder are non-consanguineal branches or sub-branches. The amount of property apportioned to each branch family has been limited to that amount of land which would yield enough food per year for a family of two adults and two children. A branch maintains a subsistence income by working for the main family, working as daylabor on days it is not required by the main family, and collecting wild vegetables. On the lunar New Year's Day each branch brings greetings and food to the main family in the morning. That night, the heads of all the branches are invited for a banquet. The seating arrangement is by status, the head of the main family and his oldest son take the most honored seats, the consanguineal branches are seated next, and then the non-consanguineal branches. Within the two groups of branches, seating order is determined by such factors as generation and wealth of the branch and education of the present head. On this day, women from the non-consanguineal branches come to do miscellaneous chores, and only consanguineal branches and relatives take part in the memorial celebrations. Although the main family no longer farms, all the branches pool their labor to transplant the rice and work in the fields of each branch in such order that the branch whose field was the first to be transplanted this year will be the last next year. After the transplanting is completed, a celebration is held at the house whose fields were first worked. The main family helps provide the food and its head attends the celebration. The status difference of the main and branch families is evident in kinship terminology as well. Members of the main family use one set of terms for members of consanguineal and well-to-do non-consanguineal branches (of which

A Farmhouse in Tatehana (Akita)

Fireplace — Inside the House (Akita)

Village of Kawairi (Okayama)

Rush Harvesting (Okayama)

entiation between consanguineal and non-consanguineal members are evident in the place at the table assigned to each, the amount of property given during and after branching, and the roles assigned when they work for the main family. Nonetheless, they have a similar status in the sense that both are in a master-servant relationship to the main family. Moreover, consanguineal branches do not look down on non-consanguineal families.

IV. LANDLORD AND TENANT

As indicated in the discussion above, the relationship between the main family and its branches is at the same time a landlord-tenant relationship. It is not a modern contractual relationship. The rent charged a tenant who is a branch member of the clan is less than that of an unrelated tenant, except when the landlord is himself a small landowner. This is one of many favors a branch-tenant receives. At the same time, tenancy does not end with payment of the rent but involves labor services to the landlord.[14] For a tenant who is also a branch family, prompt payment of rent and willing labor services are expected returns for the *on* of the landlord and main family. At the same time, if a branch is in trouble, the main family-landlord's assistance is expected.

In the large landlord-main family system, rents are generally 10–20 per cent lower; in some extreme cases as in the Adachi clan, rent was .25 *koku* for a yield of 2.3 *koku*. This may occur when, at branching, the branch leaves the land it is given in the main fam-

there are 5 out of a total of 24) and another set for the other non-consanguineal branches. For the former, grandfather is *jii*, grandmother *baba*, father (family head) *oto*, his wife *kaka*, the oldest son *anko*, oldest daughter *anekko*, and the other children are called by their names. For the latter, grandfather is *jikko*, grandmother *ba*, family head *de* or *dede*, his wife *aba*, and all sons and daughters are called by their given names. Members of a branch family call the head of the main family *otōsamanshi*, his wife *okasamanshi*, his oldest son *ansamanshi*, his junior sons *onchamanshi*, his oldest daughter *anesamanshi*, his younger daughters *ubasamanshi*, his mother *obasamanshi*. Consanguineal branches follow the practice of the main family in addressing the second group of non-consanguineal branches, while non-consanguineals use the same terms for members of the main family and consanguineal branches.

[14] Larger landlords have, in addition to branches, what is called *deiri* (literally "in and out" of their houses), who are servant-like tenants. The Ichinoseki main-family has over 20 *deiri*, who do not use their surname. In this group, a non-consanguineal sub-branch is considered a *deiri*.

ily's name. They consider this arrangement safer because as long as the main family is on a sound and secure basis, the branches will not starve; it indicates also the essential character of this kind of tenancy.

Formerly, the landlords invariably loaned rice and rice seeds. The hard labor required during rice transplanting and weeding increased the consumption of rice—which tenants could borrow from their landlord in the form of unhusked rice. The Ichinoseki main family is said to have had 800 hyō (1 hyō is about 100 lbs.) of unhusked rice in storage before World War II. In the Adachi clan, this borrowed rice is returned in the fall at an interest rate of 10 per cent. When a tenant returns the rice, he labels the rice bag with his name before he stores it in the main family's warehouse; the following year he borrows again the rice he returned the year before. The interest rate might seem exorbitantly high, but the individuals concerned do not think so. Rather than make an issue of the interest rate, they regard the main family's warehouse as their own.

One or two examples of this clan involvement in tenancy which goes beyond economic rationality may be given. In Niida, over 400 chō of the total 640 chō of cultivated land—roughly two-thirds—have been sold to merchants and money-lenders who live in Ōdate, but the traditional familial tenancy relation, i.e., between the oyakata-main family-landlord and the kokata-branch-tenant persists. Resident landlords have contributed to improving irrigation and dikes in this area where flooding has been a perennial problem and the tenants respect the landlords for such action. Tenants never consider that the landlords may be exploiting them. The Ichinoseki tenants, who are charged 30 per cent less than the usual rent, would never dream of striking for a still lower rate. At the time of the post-war land reform, when the Ichinoseki main family volunteered to release some 60 chō of land, some branch-tenants asked the main house to keep the land rather than give it up. On behalf of an absentee landlord in Ōdate another tenant said, "I simply would not be able to ask my landlord to sell the land, because he has let me use his land up to now." Many tenants are afraid of the financial burdens they would have to bear if they became independent owner-farmers; others fear that they would no longer be able to depend on the landlord and main family; still others lament the decline in status of the landlord-main family as a result of the land reform.

The village is thus founded on the *dōzoku* system and a landlord-tenant relationship. In Tatehana, until the end of the war, nine families—the three Nagasaki, Nakajima, and Kamada main families and six other families of equivalent status—maintained the political structure of the village. Among them the Nagasaki main family was the *oyakata*, and the Nakajima and Kamada main families its deputies. The authority of the village *oyakata* was supported by his position in the *dōzoku* and as a landlord. This structure was also evident in village elections, where no one outside of the landlord-main family class was expected to become a candidate for a village office; it was unlikely that even a well-qualified outsider would be elected to office. Even though an election was held, the results—which family was to take which office—were probably pre-determined. Village meetings, then, became a place to announce the village leaders' decisions. By the very act of attending and listening, the branch families and tenants helped to give the appearance that such decisions expressed the will of all the villagers. This was not limited to village politics; in all spheres of village life the main family was the pivot of the community. As long as the economic superiority of the main family-landlord lasted, those who migrated to the village had to join the *dōzoku* of a powerful main family-landlord and enter into a main-branch relationship with it; those who did not belong to a *dōzoku* must still recognize its head as the *oyakata* and assume a vassal-like relationship. Although the community which we investigated no longer manifests these ideal patterns, remnants of those patterns remain. It is not difficult to recognize the typical features of the clan, or northeastern-type, village: the predominance of one *dōzoku* in the community, the landlord-tenant relationship centering around the main family, the incorporation of the main family's tutelary gods as the gods of the *dōzoku* and of the community, and—most important—its use of a familial hierarchy as a prototype.

B)   A Community-Type Village in an
Economically Developed Area

I. A Sketch of the Village

Kawairi is a village north of a town called Niwase located half-way between two cities, Okayama and Kurashiki. This village, with its glass-windowed and tile-roofed houses, is in bright contrast to the dismal villages of Akita prefecture. Since the houses are compact and there are few trees, the visitor has a clear view of the village from its outskirts. The white walls of a number of the houses serve to symbolize the relative affluence here. Inside the houses, also, everything seems well-kept, polished, and neatly arranged, far more so than in the village houses of Akita. Since this region produces rush (which is used to make the *tatami* floor covering of Japanese houses), every room is covered with straw mats, and bare wood floors are quite rare.

The author visited the village during the New Year holidays. Had he been in the snow-covered northeast, he would have talked with villagers huddled around fireplaces in smoky rooms, but in the southwest where the winter was especially warm that year, he was able to converse with them on sun-warmed porches.

Administratively, Kawairi is part of Kibi-cho, Kibi county and is known as the birth-place of Bokudo Inukai, prime minister in 1931–2. The village is divided into three hamlets: Kawairi-honson (*honson* means "main hamlet"), Konishi, and Higashiyama. The present number of households, excluding temporary evacuees, is 153, of which 133 are farming households. More specifically, there are 65 farming households in Kawairi-honson, 44 in Konishi, and 24 in Higashiyama. The total number of 153 households represents an increase of 25 households since the beginning of the Mejii period. The 128 households registered in 1872 include 111 farming and 17 non-farming households. Of these, 66 have moved away or died out and have been replaced by 27 new households and 64 branch families.[15]

---

[15] According to the 1872 registration, the 128 households included 2 Buddhist priests; 1 Shintō priest; 4 carpenters; 4 miscellaneous employees; 1 seaman; 1

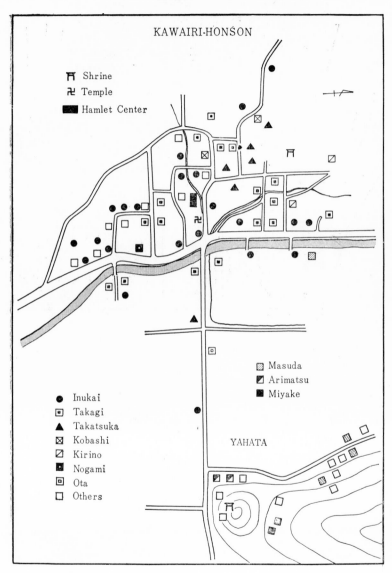

KAWAIRI-HONSON

卅 Shrine
卍 Temple
▨ Hamlet Center

● Inukai
▣ Takagi
▲ Takatsuka
⊠ Kobashi
◪ Kirino
▨ Nogami
▣ Ota
□ Others

▨ Masuda
◪ Arimatsu
■ Miyake

YAHATA

dealer each in tobacco, soy sauce, fish, grain, and cotton-batting; and one engaged both in farming and in the production of salt. Five households rented houses and five lived together with other families. The population totaled 551. The occupational distribution was as follows: agriculture 334, industry 3, trade 12, miscellaneous 21, and employed 7. The *Book of Goningumi* of 1729 recorded 89 households in the village; and an 1850 temple registry reported a population of 475. These figures indicate that both population and households increased at the end of Tokugawa Era.

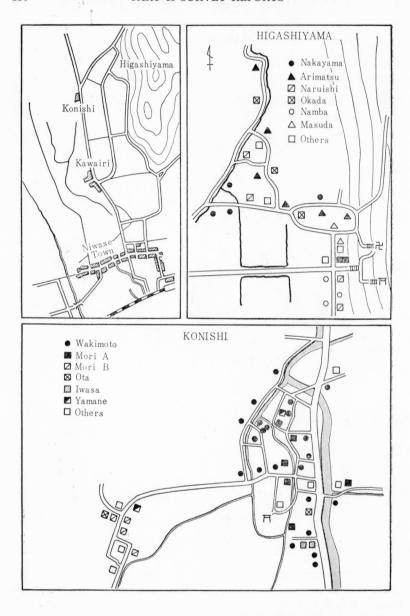

Farming consists almost entirely of rice production and rush growing; dry field crops include some vegetables for home consumption. The production of rush, a winter crop, began around 1880 and the weaving of *tatami* mats has since become a woman's occupation. Although long rush of good quality is sent to the factories, the shorter rush is still manually woven at home as a side job. As it brings in considerable income to the farmers, cultivation of the labor-intensive rush has an important bearing on the character of the village.

Rice cultivation before World War II was, on the average, 2.8–2.9 *koku* per *chō*, much higher than the overall average for the country. The number of farm implements owned by the farmers, privately and collectively, include 9 electric motors, 58 kerosene generators, 78 draft animals (including 9 horses), and 8 hand-tractors. These figures are not particularly high for a village in this region but, in comparison with northeastern villages, indicate a much higher level of prosperity.

II. The Composition of the Village

First, we will analize the characteristics of the village.

TABLE 2.   Composition of Farming Households (2)

Land cultivated (in chō)	Owner-farmer	Owner-tenant	Tenant-owner	Tenant	Total
0— .2	5	0	0	3	8
.2— .5	16	9	3	8	36
.5—1.0	18	17	16	10	61
1.0—1.5	6	7	4	4	21
1.5—2.0	0	6	1	0	7
Total	45	39	24	25	133
Percentage	34	29	18	19	100

The table indicates that more than one-half of the farm holdings range from 0.5 *chō* to 1 *chō* and that more farmers cultivate less than 0.5 *chō* than over 1 *chō*. The largest group is the owner-farmers, followed by the owner-tenant farmers. The few small farmers among the owner-farmer group are those who began to produce rice for their consumption during and after the war. Even when we exclude this somewhat unusual group, the proportion of owner-farmers is one-third and increases to over one-half when we include the owner-tenant group. The decrease in the number of tenant-farmers has been a notable postwar trend.[16]

Table 3 shows that ninety-four households own some land. Of these only three are non-cultivating landowners, owning 2.5 *chō*, 1 *chō*, and 0.25 *chō*. The statistics given here indicate that almost 70 per cent of the farming households own land. Of the landowners, three in Kawairi-honson and two in Konishi rent more than 1 *chō* of land.

TABLE 3. Land Owned by Farming Households

Ownership (in *chō*)	Landowner	Owner-tenant	Tenant	Total
0— .2	1	2	7	10
.2— .5	3	12	6	21
.5—1.0	5	27	2	34
1.0—1.5	3	15	0	18
1.5—2.0	3	3	0	6
2.0—3.0	3	0	0	3
3.0—4.0	2	0	0	2
Total	19	59	15	94

Surnames by village may be listed as follows. Kawairi-honson has 23 households with the family name Inukai,[17] divided into 6 descent lines; 16 households with the name Takagi, divided into 4 descent lines; and 6 households with the name Takatsuka, divided into 2 descent lines. There is no numerically dominant family name in the branch hamlet of Yahata. In Konishi the name Wakimoto, with 22 households, is predominant, followed by the 6 Mori households. Higashiyama is divided into small clans: 6 with the name Ari-matsu, 4 with Nakayama, 4 with Naruishi, 3 with Okada, 3 with Namba, 2 with Masuda, etc.

[16] There is a noticeable difference between the prewar and post-war periods. The transformation of non-cultivating landowners into owner-farmers is a compromise solution, as will be explained later, rather than a consequence of confiscation of their land. Many small landowners in Kawairi-honson became owner-farmers.

[17] Bokudo Inukai's family belongs to the Inukai clan in this community, but the characters used for the family name are unique. During the Tokugawa period members of his family served as district chief (peasant status, but administrator of several adjacent villages). At that time the characters of his family's name were the same as those of the other Inukai; they were changed after the beginning of the Meiji era. His sub-clan is pre-eminent. They consider themselves of a different bloodline than the rest of the Inukai.

III. The Family and Branching

The above background serves as an introduction to a more complex analysis of the family structure and the nature of branching in a communal village.

TABLE 4.   Size of Family

Number in Family	1	2	3	4	5	6	7	8	9	10	11	Total	Average
1872	8	14	20	27	26	21	7	0	4	1	0	128	4.3
1946	6	7	17	27	28	27	19	12	9	0	1	153	5.2

Table 4 shows that families of 4–6 members are most common in Kawairi; the average family size is 5.2 members. This size family is little different from that at the beginning of the Meiji period when the average was 4.3 members. When we analyze the kinship structure, we find that there are 140 families which include only lineal relatives: 64 families consisting of parents and children alone, 20 families with one grandparent, and 19 families with more than one grandparent. There are also 13 families which include collateral relatives among their members, but these relationships are not complex. There is only one family with married collateral relatives who have no children; this couple had been recently married and soon established themselves as a branch family. We may note that in 1872 there were 106 families composed exclusively of lineal kin: 53 families which numbered only parents and children, 14 which had one additional grandparent, and 6 which counted more than one additional member. There were 19 families which included collateral relatives but none of these were married. We may conclude, then, that by the end of the Tokugawa period a stable, simple form of family structure had been established.

In this area a new family may branch at a very early stage in its development, frequently immediately after marriage. This is quite unlike the northeastern village where collateral families branch out after ten years of service. About 30 per cent of the main family's land is given to a new branch family, but the total proportion of the property share increases to some 40 per cent when other properties (such as house and furniture) are included.[18] The main family is considered entitled to a larger share since it is responsible for commemorating ancestors, caring for aged parents, and perpetuating the traditional social relations. The fact that a larger share accrues to the main family does not imply any sort of a master-servant relationship.

Here, then, the branch may be established even when its head has not lived with the main family for any substantial period of time. This practice is a consequence of the relatively high productivity of this region; the traditionally lengthy service of junior sons is not required and they can maintain a fair standard of living on a comparatively small piece of land. It may further be reasoned that the severe demands of a cash economy accelerate the privation of the poorer households and hasten their emigration from the village, leaving land which may be used for new branches. We may cite the figures above as illustration: since the beginning of the Meiji era 64 branches have been established from 62 original households or, on the average, just over one branch from each household.

A change is apparent over the past eighty years in the general trend of establishing a branch. Insufficient research precludes offering precise data, but it appears that more branches were established by families in the upper stratum in the first half of the last eighty years and by the middle stratum since 1920. Lower stratum families do not have sufficient funds to establish a branch, and their junior sons are frequently sent from the village as laborers, artisans, or merchants. There has also been a growing tendency among the more well-to-do families to give their younger sons an education in preparation for work in the cities.

Junior sons in Kawairi do not appear to have a lower status than the eldest son in the daily family life. Although certain traditional expressions are occasionally used to imply their less favorable position, terms with a derogatory connotation, such as *oji* (meaning "junior son"), are not used.[19] The author's impression is that the

[18] In most cases, the head of a family determines the property division. A meeting of the family council is held only when the situation becomes complicated, and even then the main family of the *dōzoku* does not necessarily play the most important role.

[19] The term *oyakata* is sometimes heard, as an equivalent of *ani* and in contrast with *oji*. In general use, however, its meaning is practically the same as the word "eldest brother." Some elderly persons continue to say, "Second and third sons

authority of the family head is not as marked as in the north-eastern-type of village, a conclusion borne out by the responsible positions (official of the local agricultural association, etc.) held by many young and middle-aged men who are not family heads.

IV. THE DOZOKU PATTERN

The *dōzoku*, called *kabuuchi* in this area, is formed on the basis of the branching system described above. There are no grounds for the development of a master-servant relationship between the main and branch families. It is quite understandable that where there have been traditionally no large-scale landlords, the establishment of one's servant or employee as a branch house would be unlikely. As a result, the *dōzoku* consists of consanguineal members of the clan, a loosely knit kinship group in which a hierarchical structure is almost absent.

There are, of course, some exceptions. We find that one of the Takagi sub-clans gathers at the main house once a year to hold a service for their common ancestors. It is also considered proper, at various rituals and gatherings, to give the main family the most honored seats. Another branch family of one of the Takagi sub-clans was successful as a financier after the Meiji Restoration and became a landowner of 120 *chō* and a member of the prefectural assembly. As a result, the entire sub-clan abandoned Chūseiin Temple, to which they had traditionally belonged, and joined another religious organization called *Kokuchū-kai*, following the leadership of the successful branch. Since then gatherings have been held at the residence of the successful branch.[20] Special festivals may be celebrated within the clan. In general, however, strong ties between main and branch families do not extend beyond brother-brother or uncle-nephew relationships. We might say in summary that the degree of familiarity is only a little greater among clan

are, after all, hangers-on. They should not complain even if they are sent out as adopted bridegrooms; and they should not have anything to say about property division for the branch house."

[20] This house lost much of its property in the next two generations and now owns about 2.5 *chō*. What we should note, however, is that the loose main-branch relationship easily allowed a branch who had acquired power to take over the position of a main family. Some people outside the clan are also invited to its gatherings.

members, because of their common ancestry, than among the villagers as a whole. Cooperation in rice planting and collective ownership of farm implements are usually arranged among brothers, uncles, and nephews.[21] Only occasionally is the specific cooperation of clan members asked—in the event of a special prayer meeting for an ill member or a funeral, at which they gather for assistance. Even at funerals, however, the main family is assigned no specific role.

It is under such circumstances, not on the basis of clans, that *kumi* (neighborhood grouping) have been organized by families in Kawairi and Higashiyama. One exception is the *kumi* in Konishi, which are attached by name to the Wakimoto and Mori families. The Wakimoto group maintains some family traditions, legends, and festivals,[22] but does not display the typical characteristics of clan solidarity. In fact, although there was only one Wakimoto *kumi* 100 years ago, it divided as the group grew larger, the families on the east side of a certain road forming a second *kumi*. The *kumi* were not formed on the basis of the clan, but on the basis of a geographical division—which confirms the absence of hierarchical relationships between the main and branch Wakimoto families.

Although *dōzoku* solidarity is weak, it is undoubtedly a latent force in village life, for the disappearance of the clan's hierarchical structure has not meant the loss of intimate feelings of kinship among its members. We find this latent solidarity of the clan becomes manifest at election time, when the determination of village officials is made to some extent on the basis of clan.[23] It can nevertheless be asserted that the daily social life of the village is centered

[21] Cooperative rice planting is usually done in units of 2 or 3 households in Kawairi-honson. In those cases where 6 or 7 households cooperate, not only clan members but also families who cultivate nearby land join together and, thus, this type of cooperation does not occur only among *dōzoku*.

[22] According to legend, one member of the Wakimoto group was involved in a dispute with the Mori group, committed harakiri, and was deified. He is commemorated within the clan together with another deity on the last day of the third month (lunar calendar). The festival is conducted in the Buddhist tradition, and the recitation of the sutras is led by the most able member, regardless of main-branch status. Notably, there is no leadership taken by the main family at these festivals.

[23] Villagers use an expression, "there is nothing so filthy as blood," implying a high concentration of votes by clan. We heard in Kawairi-honson that agricultural association officials were often clan representatives, and that this representation was manifested more explicitly in the rice delivery quota.

around the community rather than around the clan in spite of the latter's potential influence.

V. THE FUNCTION OF KOGUMI

There used to be two groupings (*kōgumi*) in Kawairi-honson, north and south; but as the number of households increased, this division was abandoned and the households were reorganized into four groups, north, east, south, and west. The former division was the same as the agricultural association's, the latter that of the *tonari-gumi* (neighborhood association). The sub-sections of the agricultural association meet once a month; the members bring rice and perform sutra recitation at the house of the person who is in charge of the meeting. The Nichiren prayer, *namumyōhōrengekyō*, is recited since the village includes many disciples of the Nichiren sect, but non-disciples also join in. One sub-section arranges for funerals and is responsible for certain festivals at the Kawairi village shrine. The group as a whole is responsible for two village festivals, *ohimachikō* and *jochūko*. In addition, special prayers after the rice has been transplanted and door-to-door prayer visits during the summer season are made throughout Kawairi-honson.[24] It might be noted that, up until 50 years ago, prayers for the eradication of vermin were a special village event.

Yahata, a sub-*buraku* of Kawairi-honson, constitutes a neighborhood and agricultural association. In Yahata there is no group recitation of sutras, but *ohimachikō* and *shanichikō* are observed. Yahata worships the same tutelary gods as Kawairi, but does not take the duty of stewardship—perhaps because of Yahata's very recent establishment as a sub-*buraku* after a long period of subordination to the parent village.

The *kōgumi* groups of Konishi, two in the east and one in the west, function also as neighborhood associations. Here again, these units are responsible for the monthly *odaishikō* festival and the bimonthly *kinoene* festival. Each group is, in turn, responsible for the yearly festival at the tutelary shrine, as well as for the festivals of local deities. These units work together at funerals.

---

[24] Prayers are no longer offered by door-to-door solicitation; people visit the shrines themselves. In general, various traditional village ceremonies are being simplified or abandoned.

In Higashiyama, the community is also divided into two groups. Formerly known as the Arimatsu and Nakayama groups, now they simply represent geographical areas, west and east. They function concurrently as neighborhood and agricultural associations. In this hamlet, as in the others, there is monthly recitation of sutra, the bimonthly celebration of *kinoene*, and the celebration of *ohimachikō* twice a year. The entire hamlet acting as one group conducts ceremonies at the shrine of their tutelary gods: spring and autumn festivals and biannual festivals of local deities. Each house in turn takes charge of the arrangements for these events. Similarly, the whole hamlet is organized as one community for the arrangement of a villager's funeral.

VI. VILLAGE POLITICS

The *kōgumi*, then, is the basic unit in the annual hamlet festivals, and functions egalitarily under the rotating leadership of each household or some other small group. This type of association becomes apparent in inverse proportion to the solidarity of the *dōzoku*.

Village politics do not, however, operate on the communal principle, even in the so-called *kōgumi*-dominant villages. In Kawairi an influential house often acted, for a relatively long period, as hamlet representative of the local Shintō shrine. Other houses held the positions of village chief and treasurer. The village ruling group, then, has been determined to a certain extent by the status of one's house.

Although this tendency has been fading in recent years, it has not altogether disappeared, largely because of the relative stability of the village's upper stratum. It should be noted, however, that the position of village chief has been ascribed to particular houses. Our study of the position in the Taishō and Shōwa periods indicates that it was not entirely restricted to the main families. Elections have been in effect for some time, although when election time came around—at least up until the middle of the Taishō period—the incumbent official was asked to remain in office for another term. Nonetheless, the entire atmosphere was different from that which prevailed in the northeastern-type villages. Recently, in particular, one's ability has been more and more emphasized, and even a small-scale farmer may be recommended for a high position if he is competent.

Under the present system, the individuals serving as forestry managers (a part of the mountain region is collectively owned) are also village chiefs. Since they may also serve as the shrine representatives, they hold the dominant political position in the village. Elections are held every three or four years and the turnover in office is high. Since the war, the term of office for the village head, who is elected from among the village chiefs, has been limited to one year, partly in recognition of the great amount of work involved. On one occasion the village head was appointed from a house which had never even supplied anyone as forestry manager. Similar appointments have been made in other offices as well. Leadership and committee membership in the agricultural associations are not restricted to the upper stratum, and younger persons who are not yet family heads may actively participate in the agricultural association as committee members.

In Kawairi-honson, including Yahata, each of the five neighborhood groupings nominates one candidate for the offices of village chief and hamlet representative. The village chiefs become the forestry managers for the collectively owned mountain. The hamlet representatives serve concurrently as *kumi* head. The treasurer is chosen from among the five village chiefs. In the past there was a hamlet position called *kobure* to which a poor farmer was assigned. Among the present village chiefs are one landlord, two owner-farmers, one owner-tenant-farmer, and one tenant-farmer.

In Konishi, the forestry manager is elected every three years and the post alternates from house to house regardless of main-branch status. The position of shrine representative was hereditary until, many years ago, opposition was expressed. Since then the number of elected seats has increased from three to four, and elections are held every four years. The present representative of this hamlet to the whole village is an owner-farmer cultivating 1 *chō* of land, and the present hamlet chief a half-tenant farmer cultivating 1.15 *chō*.

In Higashiyama, election for forestry manager is held once every four years but the position of shrine representative is hereditary. The present hamlet representatives have all held office for the past 12 years but, socially, they belong to the lower class, one being a tenant-owner farmer cultivating .58 *chō* (renting .44 *chō*), and another an owner-tenant farmer cultivating .63 *chō* (renting .44 *chō*). In contrast, the leaders of the agricultural association are independ-

ent farmers of a relatively high status. This hamlet settles its accounts on the first of the last month of the lunar calendar when the
shrine representative, acting as accountant, collects rice to be reserved for the cost of fire prevention and for the maintenance of the
shrine. The amount which each household is to contribute is determined according to the amount of municipal tax it pays. There
are three classes of contributions, graded according to amount. (In
Higashiyama there are four or five gradations). In Konishi the
account-settlement day is the first day of the tenth month of the
lunar calendar. Various expenses for the year are covered in advance by the household in charge.

There are three persons, one in each hamlet, in charge of public
works. Their primary concern is with the historically famous
Jūnikago irrigation reservoir. The person chosen from Kawairi-
honson for this task holds the most important position, since he controls the distribution of water so that each district gets a turn every
few days.

Concomitant with these changes in village politics, the hamlet
has become increasingly independent; the traditional relative independence of the three hamlets, characterized by the worship of
their own tutelary deities, has become much more apparent. The
only reminder of village unity consists in the mountain land owned
by Kawairi village as a whole. Even this has lost much of its former
significance. The time has long passed when the village control
of use of the mountain could be used for general political control.

Kawairi village owns altogether some 11.7 chō of forest land (including .118 chō of uncultivated field), of which 1.5 cho is owned
by the honson. Income from the forest is distributed among all
the hamlet through the customary "share" system. About one-
half of the amount received by the hamlet is reserved for its own
use and the rest is distributed as dividends among all the families.
In Higashiyama, 50 per cent of the forest income is saved as a re-
serve fund, but it does not immediately become the property of the
hamlet. During the period when the forests are closed (November
3 to March 1), no one may enter them with a sickle or any other
sharp tool. Occasionally the forests will be opened during the closed
periods by special dispensation.

There is no effective control over the village community through
the management of the collectively owned forests. There is no

longer any economic hardship in purchasing fuel, and the widespread use of chemical fertilizers has reduced the need to search for
manure material. If there is any significance in the control of the
mountains, it lies merely in the pride of those households who are
shareholders and their enjoyment of the dividends. The branch
family may become shareholders upon consultation with the forestry
manager. When one branch family joined the corporation in 1943,
the admission fee was ¥30. Membership is in some cases extended
beyond branch families, i.e. through affinal relatives, since the admission qualification has not been strict.

The following are the regulations for the collectively owned
forests:

1. The collective forest shall be administered by the representative
   of Kawairi village.
2. Those who seek membership in the collective ownership shall
   apply to the said representative and pay the agreed admission
   fee.
3. Ownership shall be restricted to those households which joined
   the corporation when the collective forests were first established
   in the early Meiji period. It may be extended to their branch
   families.
4. Any member who moves from Kawairi forsakes the right of
   membership.
5. Ownership will be restored to those who move out of Kawairi
   but return and live there for more than one year.
6. In case of the extinction of a member household, the membership
   right may be passed on to any of its kin who has lived more than
   three years in Kawairi, provided that due procedures are completed within twenty years after the extinction.
7. The collective forests shall not be divided; the purpose is to re-
   serve them for descendants of the member families. No payment
   shall be made upon a member's secession.

The list of members attached to these regulations shows the following membership composition: 66 in Kawairi-honson (2 new
members in 1940, 1 in 1943), 44 in Konishi (2 new members in
1940), 25 in Higashiyama (4 new members in 1940, 1 in 1943).

Migration into the village is not difficult. The story is told of a
farmer who had come as a laborer to the village. He entertained
the neighborhood group members with dinner and *sake,* invited his

younger brother to work for him, took a wife, secured tenant land, and built a house with the help of the neighborhood group. Thus his household became completely independent. There was no prejudicial treatment against the farmer because of his laborer's status. In this case, the younger brother was not so prudent, and there was some disapproving talk, but no more. The elder brother was cautious but he by no means felt subordinate to his former master or strange in his new village life. We observe here a great difference from what we know about outside laborers attempting to find a place in the community in northeastern Japan, where they can succeed only by the grace of a *dōzoku*.

In summary, the village is partitioned into several hamlets, each of which comes directly under the administrative village. The relative independence of each household within a hamlet increases as the socio-political structure of the village becomes more flexible with the increasing importance of the communal principle. Moreover, integration based on communal organization is itself becoming more significant, *i.e.*, while the social relationship of each household may very well expand beyond the limit of the hamlet or village to which it belongs, at the same time the sphere of practical daily life is more and more confined to the immediate neighborhood.

VII. Social Characteristics

It is hardly necessary to assert that differences exist among these theoretically equal farm households. Social stratification within the village has been observed since the beginning of the Meiji period. The extent of occupational differentiation seen in the 1872 Registration does not exist in the northeastern-type village; it indicates social stratification and the poorer farmers' dissatisfaction with agriculture. The Itakura clan's exploitation at the end of the Tokugawa Shogunate has given us the *taruda* practice. There were some instances when the desertion of farmers had to be made up by migrant workers from other villages known as *debyakushō*.[25] They

---

[25] *Taruda* refers to the practice of giving *sake* to anyone to whom the right of cultivation is transferred. *Debyakusho* (and also *deyashiki*) refers to migrant workers who were brought in, mainly from the western parts of the prefecture, to reinforce the reduced farm population. It is said that they were provided with a rice paddy of .6 *chō*, a bull, and lodging facilities.

were naturally denigrated as a low status group. An old farmer told us, recollecting his childhood days, that these migrant workers were addressed without any title of courtesy and had to cringe back in the corner at village meetings. Until the end of the Meiji period the lower status tenant-farmer group was not treated on a par with the owner-farmer or landlord groups which monopolized the higher official positions; at that time the lower status groups were ill-advised to even attempt to air their grievances. Fortunately, these individuals are now considered full-fledged members of the village, discrimination appearing only in marriage. As we have seen, tenancy continues today; and although the number of landleasing farm households is considerable, the size of their holdings and their power has diminished greatly. The leaser-leasee relationship has been defined in terms of economic power and not in terms of some feudal status bondage, which would have tied the tenant farmer to the landowner. Recently, as farmers have gained more and more independence, landlordism as such has lost its significance. In spite of status differences, the majority of farming houses are conscious of their relative independence. Today, the *kōgumi* which has ancient roots is even more important than in the past.

How did this village take on such a community structure? It would seem that the primary factor is the absence of large land-owners. *Dōzoku* solidarity was thus inhibited and the development of the *kōgumi* organization promoted, allowing little chance for domination or subordination in relationships between landowner and tenant farmer. Although stratification resulted in a little more land for the wealthy farmers, it did not lower the position of tenant farmers, since most of the wealthy farmers were, after all, dependent on their farm rent income.[26]

[26] The farm rent (per .1 *chō*) before amelioration was *ca.* 1.4 to 1.7 *koku* when the land was exceptionally productive. For long-term tenants it was *ca.* 1.3 *koku*. After amelioration it was set at 1.1–1.4 *koku*. In the event of a bad crop, tenants may confer with the landlords and appeal for rent reduction. Though farm rent is not low, there is no other obligation to the landowner. A high mobility in landowner-tenant relationships prevents the rigid subordination of tenant farmers. In this village, furthermore, the landowner is expected to consult his tenant when selling his land, whether or not the latter buys it. Elections are little affected by one's relationship with a certain landowner, except for lone farmers without any *dōzoku* ties. Landowners, therefore, cannot dominate the village by their economic power alone. Landowners themselves own only small pieces of land, and those who live in an adjacent hamlet do not own

Second, the relatively high agricultural productivity allowed each farmer to be independent on even a small piece of land. At the same time, because a large labor supply was not required by one household, branch families could be established at an early stage, and on a basis more or less equal to the main family. Consequently the usual *dōzoku* solidarity has not been fostered even in limited aspects of village life.

Third, we must consider the high degree of infiltration of a money economy into the village. Generally speaking, the penetration of a cash economy promotes stratification and drives marginal farmers off the land or increases their destitution. In this village, which is close to several industrial cities, those who are not able to live comfortably leave with no hesitation, and new branch houses are established in their place. Such mobility eliminates status traditions based on personal ties. Moreover, if farming does not offer adequate compensation, farmers can seek employment elsewhere for added income. Where there is no opportunity for supplementary employment except as a day-laborer, the poor marginal farmer group has no choice but to remain subject to the village's upper stratum or to their respective employers; but in this village no one need be forced into such a humiliating position.

Finally, we must remember that rush is produced as a cash crop in the area. Even though rush cultivation requires hard labor, it brings in a much greater income than wheat or barley, common winter crops in southwestern Japan, and further income can be expected by processing harvested rush. This encourages the independence of the marginal farmers. The villagers' feeling of equality is generated by their higher standard of living.

more than 10 *chō*. Because landowners are, on the average, small-scale and because there is no concentration of land in the hands of large absentee landowners, no class-conscious tenant movement has developed.

INDEX

CHINA

Absentee landlord, 83, 92
Administrative system, 91–2
Agricultural hamlet, 81
Agricultural laborer, 84
Agricultural population, 13
Agricultural productivity, 3–4

Chiatang, 87
Chienhui, 85
Clan, 4, 16–8, 83, 85–8: chief, 16–7, 87; consciousness, 88; exogamy, 4, 86; officials, 16; property, 18, 83, 87; shrine, 16, 87; solidarity, 17–8; structure of, 16–8; system, 85–8
Collateral relatives, 14, 85
Common property ownership, 15
Communal autonomy, 23
Communist indoctorination, 8
Communist revolution, 7
Creek, 81, 84
Crop-watching association, 21

Debt, 85, 88
Document of property partition, 86

Earth god, 21, 89
Education, 92
Eldest son, 14, 86–7
Employed laborer, 84
Equal division of property, 4, 18
Extended family system, 15
Exogamy, 4, 18, 86

Familism, 24–5
Family, 13–6, 24, 85–6: characteristics of, 13–6; head, 85–6; principal, 16; status, 24; system, 86
Family property, 14, 85; common ownership of, 14
Farmer, 19, 82–5, 88, 90–1: full-time, 83; lower-class, 85, 88; marginal, 84; middle-class, 84–5, 88; owner, 82–3; owner-tenant, 19, 83; part-time, 83; petty, 84–6; poor, 90; tenant, 19, 82–3; wealthy, 84, 90–1
Farm house, 81
Farming household, 83–4
Farm rent, 83, 90
Festival, 89
Feudalism, 25
Filial piety, 87
Full-time farmer, 83
Funeral, 85, 87: expence, 87

Genealogical records, 18, 87
Generation, 16–7, 24, 87
Gentry, 5, 22, 24
Girl, 86

Hamlet, 81
House, 81
Hired farmer, 85

Irrigation, 84
Inheritance, 4, 86

INDIA

JAPAN